Mystical Tradition:
Judaism, Christianity, and Islam
Part I

Professor Luke Timothy Johnson

THE TEACHING COMPANY ®

PUBLISHED BY:

THE TEACHING COMPANY
4151 Lafayette Center Drive, Suite 100
Chantilly, Virginia 20151-1232
1-800-TEACH-12
Fax—703-378-3819
www.teach12.com

ISBN 1-59803-467-7

Luke Timothy Johnson, Ph.D.

Robert W. Woodruff Professor of New Testament and Christian Origins
at Candler School of Theology, Emory University

Luke Timothy Johnson, Ph.D., is the Robert W. Woodruff Professor of New Testament and Christian Origins at Candler School of Theology, Emory University, in Atlanta, Georgia. Born in 1943, he was a Benedictine monk from the ages of 19 to 28. He received a B.A. in Philosophy from Notre Dame Seminary in New Orleans, an M.Div. in Theology from Saint Meinrad School of Theology in Indiana, and an M.A. in Religious Studies from Indiana University before earning a Ph.D. in New Testament Studies from Yale University in 1976.

Professor Johnson taught at Yale Divinity School from 1976 to 1982 and at Indiana University from 1982 to 1992 before accepting his current position at Emory. He is the author of 20 books, including *The Writings of the New Testament: An Interpretation* (3rd edition, 2003), which is used widely as a textbook in seminaries and colleges. He has also published several hundred articles and reviews. He is currently at work on several books, including one on the Christian creed, one on the future of Catholic biblical scholarship, and one on the influence of Greco-Roman religion on Christianity.

Professor Johnson has taught undergraduates, as well as master's level and doctoral students. At Indiana University, he received the President's Award for Distinguished Teaching, was elected a member of the Faculty Colloquium on Excellence in Teaching, and won the Brown Derby Teaching Award and the Student Choice Award for teaching. At Emory, he has twice received the On Eagle's Wings Excellence in Teaching Award, and in 2007, he received the Candler School of Theology Outstanding Service Award. In 1997 and 1998, he was a Phi Beta Kappa visiting scholar, speaking at college campuses across the country.

Professor Johnson is married to Joy Randazzo. They share 7 children, 13 grandchildren, 4 great-grandchildren, and a Yorkshire terrier named Bailey. Professor Johnson's other courses for The Teaching Company are: *The Apostle Paul*; *Early Christianity: The Experience of the Divine*; *Great World Religions: Christianity* (2nd edition); *Jesus and the Gospels*; *Practical Philosophy: The Greco-Roman Moralists*; and *The Story of the Bible*.

Table of Contents

Mystical Tradition: Judaism, Christianity, and Islam
Part I

Professor Biography i
Course Scope 1
Lecture One   A Way into the Mystic Ways of the West.......... 4
Lecture Two   Family Resemblances and Differences 18
Lecture Three   The Biblical Roots of Western Mysticism 32
Lecture Four   Mysticism in Early Judaism 46
Lecture Five   Merkabah Mysticism...................................... 60
Lecture Six   The Hasidim of Medieval Germany.................. 73
Lecture Seven   The Beginnings of Kabbalah............................ 86
Lecture Eight   Mature Kabbalah—*Zohar* 99
Lecture Nine   Isaac Luria and Safed Spirituality 113
Lecture Ten   Sabbatai Zevi and Messianic Mysticism........ 126
Lecture Eleven   The Ba'al Shem Tov
                     and the New Hasidism 139
Lecture Twelve   Mysticism in Contemporary Judaism............. 152
Timeline 166
Glossary 175
Bibliography 185

Mystical Tradition: Judaism, Christianity, and Islam

Scope:

The greatest human ambition is to seek God, and the only true tragedy is failing to become a saint. These are the convictions of the men and women that others often call mystics, although they more often speak of themselves simply as seekers, servants, lovers, and disciples. They are the most passionately personal practitioners of religion. Their chosen instrument is prayer. Their lifelong quest is to experience the living God. They regard their search for God as the expression of what is most authentic within themselves, as well as the greatest service they could pay to their fellow humans: If the greatest part of humanity is blind, is it not the truest form of love to show them a glimpse of light?

This course examines the magnificent tradition of mysticism within the major Western religions of Judaism, Christianity, and Islam. These religions are usually thought of in terms of external observance—doctrines, laws, rituals—rather than in terms of intense prayer experiences or forms of contemplation. In fact, however, all three monotheistic religions of the West have robust and complex mystical traditions. Indeed, those who follow the path of contemplation would argue that their way of being Jewish, Christian, or Muslim was the purest realization of that religion's essence.

For whatever reason, mystics are also responsible for some of the most impressive literature produced by their respective religions. Mystics authored interpretations of Scripture, theological treatises, sermons, meditations, letters, stories, and poems, and all of them testify to the fact that a fervent love of the divine—and a search for contact with the inexpressible—does not require the rejection of literary art or the love of human beauty. Some mystical literature, indeed, is suffused with an intense eroticism that fuses human and divine passion in a single fire.

An introduction to the varieties of mystical literature through the ages, and to the great spiritual teachers within each tradition who composed such writings, is an important element in this course. It is impossible to appreciate the richness of the mystical way without some direct contact with the words that were forged out of the experience of prayer. As much as possible, then, this course will use the words of the mystics themselves.

A major goal of this course, however, is to create a context for those words. First, it places mystical literature squarely within the exoteric forms of each religion. There are, to be sure, clear similarities in mysticism across religious traditions, but it is worth asking about the forms it adopts within specific beliefs and practices. Second, despite being a highly personal form of religious sensibility, mysticism has flourished most within well-developed and firm communities of shared practice. Jewish mystics found their place within a community of halachic observance; Christian mystics are frequently located within monastic communities; and in Islam, Sufi fellowships support the practices that enable a personal quest for the divine. The tensions—creative and destructive—inherent in an esoteric appropriation of an exoteric tradition require attention, but such tensions exist because of a state of mutual dependence. Third, even though mysticism tends to exist with little reference to outside events, it is often important to situate specific forms of mystical expression within historical and social circumstances.

The course begins with three ground-laying presentations. The first takes up the matters of definition (what do we mean by "mysticism"?) and scope (literature rather than direct experience) and raises some preliminary questions (for example, why do mystics write at all?). The second sketches the family resemblances and squabbles within the three traditions that share common roots, as well as a history of controversy. The third examines the most important of the common roots, namely, the biblical basis for mystical experience and symbolism.

Lectures Four through Eleven trace the historical stages of mysticism in the Jewish tradition, beginning with the inchoate expressions of the Hellenistic period, moving through Merkabah and Kabbalah, and ending with Hasidism. Lectures Thirteen through Twenty-Four provide a similar survey of mysticism within Christianity, beginning with the figures of Jesus and Paul, then considering the radical challenge to exoteric Christianity posed by Gnosticism, before examining major movements and figures in the Orthodox, Catholic, and Protestant forms of Christianity. Lectures Twenty-Six through Thirty-Four are devoted to mysticism in Islam, beginning with Muhammad as mystic, then sketching the exoteric form of the "House of Islam" and the mystical character of the Shi'a, before surveying the development of Sufism, with special attention to its great early teachers and masters in the West (North Africa) and East

(India and Persia). At the end of each unit (Lectures Twelve, Twenty-Five, and Thirty-Five) are presentations devoted to contemporary expressions of mysticism within each of the three traditions. Although the greater part of this course is devoted to foundational figures of the distant past, it is necessary to note, however briefly, the continuation of the same pilgrimage toward God in the present.

The final lecture of the course will take up two questions that, in one way or another, run through all the preceding presentations. The first question concerns the truth claims of mystics: Are they merely writers of considerable charm, or are they in touch with what is most real? Are they self-deluded fools or the wisest of humans? Are they tragically mistaken, or are they, in fact, witnesses to a truth hidden to others because of distraction and denial? The second question concerns the viability of mysticism in the contemporary world: Will it survive the onslaughts of aggressive secularism, or will it survive and possibly even surmount a world shaped around the denial of what it holds most dear?

Lecture One
A Way into the Mystic Ways of the West

Scope:

Understanding the mystical path in Western religions begins with some preliminary questions and basic definitions of terms: What do we mean by "religious experience," "religion," "mysticism," and "prayer"? Defining these terms leads, in turn, to a consideration of the premises concerning the construction of reality shared by mystics: What is the relation of the exoteric to the esoteric? What is the relation of mystical experience and mystical writing? What is the range of evidence available for the study of mysticism in Judaism, Christianity, and Islam? This opening presentation then sketches the logic of the entire sequence of lectures.

Outline

I. This lecture begins with a set of opening questions, the answers to which can provide some guidance for the remaining 35 lectures.

   A. Is "mysticism" another term for the irrational and, therefore, undeserving of serious scholarly analysis?

      1. To some extent, the question arises from loose popular usage that links mysticism, mystery, magic, mystification, and even self-delusion.

      2. But it also arises from the rationalistic bias of contemporary science and technology, which equates the verifiable with the true and the "mystical" with the avoidance of real life.

      3. To some extent, the same charge can be made against all religion and every claim concerning reality beyond the empirical.

      4. Mystics claim, however, to be in contact with what is most real, with that which is not irrational but super-rational, and that a reduction of truth to the pragmatic and provable is tragic.

   B. Are mystics, then, always extraordinary adepts constantly in a state of ecstasy or constantly having visions?

      1. We shall see that mysticism does, in fact, include such extraordinary religious types as visionaries and ecstatics.

2. But the term can also be used to include all those who seek a personal and passionate devotion to the divine and need not involve psychic fireworks. Mysticism embraces every social class, level of intelligence, and degree of emotional health.

3. We can appreciate the greatness of music through the genius of a Mozart, but we can see, too, that piano students struggling with simple tunes also participate in music. In the same way, the great mystics and visionaries show us the range of what is possible in the life of devotion to God while including those at a much lower scale of performance.

C. Isn't mysticism really the distinctive quality in Eastern religions, such as Hinduism and Buddhism?

1. It is true that Judaism, Christianity, and Islam are usually associated with external observance of religious law, ritual, and morality within a community.

2. But all three traditions have a long and robust tradition of mysticism, whose practitioners claim to represent those religions in their essence.

3. We should also note that Asian religions have as great a commitment to the same elements of law, ritual, and morality as do the religions of the West.

II. We can move even further into the subject matter by defining some basic terms that will recur in the course, keeping in mind that all these definitions are the instructor's and not necessarily universally held.

A. We begin by defining "religious experience" with a basic definition from Joachim Wach: "Religious experience is a response of the whole person to what is perceived as ultimate, characterized by a peculiar intensity, and issuing in appropriate action."

1. The element of "response" indicates the conviction that religious experience is not fantasy or self-generated.

2. "The whole person" indicates that religious experience is not merely a matter of ideas, or of will, or of emotions but involves the whole person, including the body.

3. "Perceived as ultimate" points both to the subjective character of religious experience and its claim to "transcendence."

4. "Characterized by peculiar intensity" points to the aspect of "realness"; religious experience is not something vague or uncertain but definite and impressive.

5. The "appropriate action" is the organization of life in a new manner around the experience.

B. A "religion" is a way of life organized around experiences and convictions concerning ultimate power.

1. The way of life involves a community of shared practice: Ritual and myth, doctrine, sacred books, and codes of morality are all ways of mediating the power of religious experience in indirect and nonthreatening ways.

2. One way of viewing mysticism is as the individual search for unmediated contact with ultimate power.

C. The term "mysticism" retains some elements of its Greek etymology.

1. The *mystes* is one who has been initiated into a cult and, thereby, has access to status and lore not available to the uninitiated.

2. The term "mystic" is usually used for an individual rather than a group and suggests entry into a new realm and access to knowledge not available to others and not fully expressible in ordinary speech.

D. In general, the term "prayer" refers to the practice of human communication with respect to the divine.

1. Community prayer most often takes a verbal form in petition, praise, confession, vow, or hymn.

2. The prayer of mystics may involve words but often transcends speech, either through ecstatic utterance or silence.

3. Contemplation, meditation, or the Prayer of Silence are almost universally attested as mystical practices.

III. A number of questions will preoccupy us as we study the mystical tradition in Western religions.

A. What construction of reality is presupposed by the practice of mysticism?

1. A dimension of being that is greater and truer than that visible to the senses exists.

2. Some capacity within humans enables them to gain access to that dimension of reality.

3. Those who have already gained such access can instruct others in the methods of gaining it.

B. What is the relationship between the exoteric (outer) and esoteric (inner) in mysticism?

1. How does mysticism relate to the outward observances shared by a religious community? To what extent does it affirm or slight the outward?

2. How does the inner experience of contemplation or ecstasy find expression exoterically in the symbolism of gesture or language?

C. Why do some mystics write about their experiences, and why do they write what they do?

1. Certainly, many mystics never write, and indeed, the logic of mysticism tends away from literary expression.

2. Some mystical writing serves as instruction; some, as speculation; and some, it seems, as a medium of experience.

D. What sources are available for the study of mysticism in the religions of the West?

1. We have an abundance of literature from Judaism, Christianity, and Islam in English translation, including tractates, poetry, instructions, wisdom writings, prayer, and narratives.

2. English sources represent only a small portion of the works in the original languages of Hebrew, Greek, and Latin, as well as modern European languages, Arabic, and Persian.

3. The instructor in this course has a grasp of some of these languages (Hebrew, Greek, Latin, French, and German) but not others, most notably, the most important languages for the Islamic tradition (Arabic and Persian).

IV. We will approach this course in a fundamentally chronological sequence for each of the traditions in turn, beginning with Judaism, then Christianity, then Islam.

A. The opening lectures provide a necessary framework with a review of the exoteric traditions and the biblical basis of mystical symbolism.

B. The treatment of mysticism within each tradition seeks to make clear both what is distinctive and what is common.

1. The main focus is on mystical literature as produced by great masters within the traditions.
2. Through the examination of this literature, we will explore analytic questions concerning mysticism.

C. Although the focus is on the classical sources of the past, each unit concludes with some consideration of the practice of mysticism today.

D. The course ends with a set of questions concerning the truth of mystical claims and the viability of mystical practice in a secular world.

Recommended Reading:

Smith, M. "The Nature and Meaning of Mysticism," in *Understanding Mysticism*, pp. 19–25.

Questions to Consider:

1. Consider the ways that mystical experience is necessarily "mediated," both by the symbols made available by an exoteric tradition and by the constraints of literary composition.

2. Discuss the characteristic of religious experience as "peculiarly intense": What forms might this intensity take?

Lecture One—Transcript
A Way into the Mystic Ways of the West

Welcome to this Teaching Company course on mysticism in the great monotheistic religions of the West: Judaism, Christianity, and Islam. My name is Luke Johnson. I am not, I assure you, a mystagogue who will initiate you into the mysteries. Nor am I a spiritual master who can offer you a higher state of cosmic awareness. I am a scholar of religion with a particular interest in religious experience. And my goal in this course is to provide you with some sense of the breadth and the depth of the claims to the direct experience of the divine in these traditions.

This first presentation begins with a set of opening questions, the answers to which can provide some guidance for the remaining 35 presentations. An appropriate entry into the subject is provided by a set of three basic questions. The first is: Is "mysticism" simply another term for the irrational and, therefore, undeserving of scholarly analysis? To some extent, this question arises from loose popular usage that links mysticism, mystery, magic, mystification, and even self-delusion. To be mystical means to be out of touch. The mystic is, well, mystified. But the question also arises from the rationalistic bias of contemporary science and technology, which tends to equate the true with what is verifiable and the mystical with the avoidance of real life. If what is real is what is measurable, then any claim to be in contact with what is immeasurable, that is infinite, is obviously delusional.

And, indeed, the same charge could be made, to some extent, against any religious confession. All religion says that it is seeking contact with what is beyond the empirically verifiable, and indeed, many important statements in our ordinary life make the same kind of claim. The statement "I love you" is scarcely available to an obvious examination for its truth value. Mystics, however, claim just the opposite to be the case. They claim to be in contact with what is most real, not with what is not irrational—that is, against reason—but the super-rational—that is, that goes beyond what is available to the ordinary processes of human reason. They say that reducing truth to the pragmatic and the provable is itself tragic. Their claim, then, challenges the ordinary, dominant epistemologies, or theories of knowledge, of our age. And they, in fact, reverse the charge of delusion. Those who claim only the visible as real are the ones, say the mystics, who are most out of touch.

Second question: Are mystics, then, always extraordinary adepts, constantly in a state of ecstasy or constantly having visions? Is the study of mysticism, in effect, the study of what is psychically paranormal? We shall see, in fact, that mysticism does include such extraordinary religious types as visionaries and ecstatics. We shall hear of highly detailed visions of heaven and of the future. We shall hear of flashes of light. We shall hear claims of being in the body or out of the body. But the term "mysticism" ought to include also all those who seek a personal and passionate devotion to the divine and need not include such psychic fireworks. It's a personal devotion to the divine. It is something undertaken by the individual. It is a passionate devotion. It is considered by the devotee to be more important than anything else. It is a devotion; that is, it requires commitment, consistency, and practice. Many of the great mystical writers never claim any of these psychic fireworks, such as visions or states of ecstasy. We will see also that mysticism embraces virtually every social class: peasants as well as nobles, the poor as well as the wealthy, women as well as men. It embraces every level of intelligence, from the most highly intelligent scholars to those who are illiterate, and—of great interest—every degree of emotional health. We will see that sometimes, mysticism is correlated to states of neurosis, but other times, we will see that mystics display the most robust and radiant good psychological health. So just as one can appreciate the greatness of music through the genius of a Mozart— and perhaps that genius ought to be the norm by which all music is measured—we would also admit that the beginning piano student who is struggling through ordinary five-finger exercises also participates in the great world of music. In the same way, the great mystics and visionaries perhaps show us the range of what is possible to the life of devotion to God, but at the same time, mysticism includes those at a much lower scale of performance.

A third opening question: Isn't mysticism really the distinctive quality in Eastern religions, like Hinduism and Buddhism? Aren't we, in effect, looking in the wrong place when we look at Judaism, Christianity, and Islam for mysticism? It is true that these Western traditions are usually associated with external observance of religious law, ritual, and morality within a community. Our first image of a Jew, Christian, or Muslim is not someone sitting in the lotus position but of someone who is terribly busy about religious works. We tend to think of these Western religions in terms of being active, rather than contemplative. But we will find in this course that all three traditions have a long and robust tradition of mysticism, whose practitioners can and have made the claim to represent those religions in their essence. In other words, it's not a question of whether or not a Jew, a Christian, or a Muslim can be allowed to be a mystic. Their claim is that Jewish Mysticism, Christian Mysticism, and Islamic Mysticism really represent the essence of what those three traditions are about. And by the way, we should add that Asian religions also have as great a commitment to the same elements of law, ritual, and morality as do the so-called religions of the West.

Having treated those opening questions, I would like to move more deeply into the subject matter of this course by defining some basic terms that will recur throughout. Please remember that these definitions are mine. They are by no means universally held. Some students of religion, for example, shy away from even speaking about religious experience. They either don't believe it exists or they think it is too difficult to define. I am not so shy. I both think that such a thing exists and that, although it is difficult to define, it is possible at least to make a good effort.

I begin with defining "religious experience," and I use here the basic definition of the formerly great sociologist of religion at the University of Chicago, Joachim Wach: "Religious experience is a response of the whole person to what is perceived as ultimate, characterized by a peculiar intensity, and issues in appropriate action." I will now take each of those terms and try to explain what each part of that definition means.

The first element is the "note of response." This indicates that for the religious person, such experience is not a matter of fantasy, of self-hypnosis. It is not self-generated, and it doesn't depend on having some particularly good dope. It is, rather, a response to something that is real. There is an other to whom I respond, even if that other is my higher self. The phrase "the whole person" indicates that religious experience is not merely a matter of ideas, or of the will, or of feelings but involves the whole person, including the body. So it is not a matter simply of religious ideas—"I believe that there is a God," as in a creed. It is not merely a matter of volition—"I want to be holy." Nor is it a matter simply of feeling—"I feel fear when I am in this space." It can and does involve all of these dimensions of the human person—the mind, the will, the feelings, and the body—not necessarily all together and all the time, but in principle, all of them are involved in religious experience.

The phrase "perceived as ultimate" touches on two important topics. The first is this: The term "perceived" gets us to the inevitably subjective character of religious experience. It is my perception of what is ultimate. What I perceive to be ultimate may not be what you perceive to be ultimate, but it is essentially a deeply subjective starting point. But it is the perception of what is ultimate, and this leads us to the religious term "transcendence." The religious person thinks of himself or herself as experiencing something that goes beyond; that's what the word "transcendence" means. It goes beyond what is beautiful, or useful, or pleasurable to me. It is in another category altogether.

The fourth element in this definition is that religious experience is "characterized by a peculiar intensity." This is the element of realness in this experience. It is not vestigial. It's not vague. It is not something that I might have misunderstood. I may not be able to say what it is that I have experienced, but I can clearly state that I have experienced something; something has happened to me.

And finally, the phrase "issues an appropriate action"—this gets at the difference between an aesthetic experience, in which I listen to the music of Mozart and I'm totally enthralled by it. Listening to the music of Mozart does not necessarily reorganize my life around Mozart, and this is what genuine religious experience does: It reorganizes my life, even down to the fundamental axes of time and space, around what I perceive to be ultimate power.

And that leads me to the second term to define, namely, "religion." If religious experience is a response to what is perceived as ultimate power, issuing an appropriate action, then a religion is simply a way of life organized around such experiences and convictions concerning ultimate power. This way of life involves a community of shared practice. Individuals don't have their own religion. A religion is a way of life shared by many around certain ultimate experiences and convictions, and embodied communities have various ways to mediate religious experience. They have rituals, things that they do repetitively. They have myths, stories that they tell. They have doctrines or beliefs. They have sacred books. They have codes of morality. All of these aspects of religion mediate or seek to mediate the power of religious experience in indirect and, therefore, nonthreatening ways. One of the religious functions of ritual is to enable people to participate in what is perceived as powerful without being destroyed by it. Viewed in this way, within the framework of a religion, mysticism can be seen as the individual's search for unmediated contact with ultimate power. So if the entire community is working with these mediated forms of ritual, and myth, and doctrine, and morality, the mystic is one who takes it upon himself or herself individually to make direct contact with that ultimate power. It need not be in opposition to the mediating forms, but it seeks to go beyond it—again, to transcend such mediation.

The term "mysticism" retains some elements of its Greek etymology and its use in the cults that were called the Greek mysteries. The *mystes* is one who is initiated into a cult and, thereby, gains access to a status and lore, a body of knowledge, that is not available to the uninitiated. The *mystes*, the mystic, is one who goes to a place guided by another, has contact in that place with what is ultimate, and is, thereby, changed. So the term "mystic," against that background, is usually used for an individual rather than a group and suggests entry into a new realm and access to knowledge not available to others and not fully expressible in ordinary speech. The ancient mysteries had what was called the *disciplina arcana*, the discipline of secrecy: that one was forbidden to reveal to those who were not initiated what exactly one experienced in contact with the ultimate.

The final term to define is "prayer." Prayer, in general, is the practice of human communication with respect to the divine. Community prayer, prayer within a religion, most often takes a verbal form. It is spoken usually and can consist of petition, praise, confession, vows, or hymns. All of us are familiar with the various verbal forms of religious speech. The prayer of mystics sometimes involves words but often transcends ordinary speech in one of two ways, either through some form of ecstatic speech—that is, speaking in tongues, recitation of the divine names, the repetition of, let us say, the "Jesus Prayer," rapidly correlating words with breathing, all of these techniques—or it may also consist simply in silence—contemplation, meditation, or the prayer of silence. Recollection is almost universally attested as an element in mysticism. Ordinary reality enables us to speak in ordinary ways. The claim to have contact with what is extraordinary means that speech itself becomes dislocated, either in the form of ecstatic speech or by being struck silent.

A number of questions will preoccupy us as we study the mystical tradition in Western religions. The first question is: What construction of reality is presupposed by the practice of mysticism? It's obviously one very different than that we find in contemporary commerce and Consumerism. The first premise is that there is a dimension of being greater and truer than that visible to the senses, that this is real. Muslims speak of *al-haqq*, the "real." It is real. It is greater. It's not transitory but permanent. It is truer; it makes real knowledge available, not simply opinion. The second premise is that there's something within the human that enables them to gain access to that dimension of reality. Whether it is the soul, whether it is spirit, whether it is a spark of the divine light, something in humans enables them to enter into contact with that which is more real than what is seen. And thirdly, the premise is that those who have already gained access to such a level of being can instruct others in the methods of gaining it. Mysticism includes both the experience and instruction in that experience.

Another question: What is the relationship between the exoteric and the esoteric in mysticism? First, let me explain the two terms; I'll be using them very often in this course. "Exoteric" means that which is outward. It's visible; it's external; it is open to all. It is public. It is, for example, ritual. The "esoteric" is inward. It is hidden. It is invisible. It is more secret. The question is: How do the exoteric and esoteric work in mysticism? There's two ways of putting the question. The first is: How does mysticism relate to the outward observances shared by a religious community? To what extent do mystics either affirm or slight what other religious people are doing? And we will see very different responses to that. We will see sometimes that exoteric religion tends to shun the esoteric. We will see at other times that the esoteric practitioners have contempt for the exoteric. It's an uneasy sort of relationship. But the second way of posing the question is: How do the inner experiences of contemplation or ecstasy find outward expression in the symbols of gesture or language? And so we find that even if an experience is unmediated, even if psychically I come into some contact with what is ultimate, if I am going to express this experience to others, then I must use the exoteric symbols that are made available by a particular religious tradition. So esoteric and exoteric are always related in some fashion. And I'm going to argue in the course of these lectures that, in fact, they have a healthy tension that operates between them.

Another question: Why do mystics write, and why do they write what they do? Certainly, far more mystics never write; the huge majority of people who practice mystical prayer are not authors. But for those who do create literary works, it's not quite clear why they do. Some mystical writing certainly serves as instruction to teach others the way; some serves as speculation; involves the attempt to put into some ordered fashion what one experienced in prayer. And even—and I'm going to suggest this at several points in the course— sometimes writing, it seems to me, even serves as a medium of expression. That is, the mystic actually has experiences through the act of writing so that the writing of visions is itself a medium of the visionary.

A final question that we should consider is the question of sources: What sources are available for the study of mysticism in the religions of the West? There is an abundance of literature from all three traditions in English translation: tractates, poetry, instructions, wisdom writings, prayer, and narratives. I should mention that many of these have only recently been made available. You will notice in your outlines and in your recommended readings that I make frequent reference to volumes in a series called *The Classics of Western Spirituality*, which began publication around 1978 and continues. Many of the great mystical writings have only been made available in English translation relatively recently, which means that a course like this would be possible only relatively recently. But a more significant observation is that these English sources represent only a tiny portion of the works in the original languages of the mystics, only a small portion. Generally, what we see when we do a course like this is what might be called the top 10, or the hit parade, of mystical works, those that everybody recognizes are extremely important and so they rush to edit and translate them. But there are vast amounts of literature in the original languages of Hebrew, Greek, Latin, modern European languages, Arabic, and Persian that simply remain unedited and untranslated and, therefore, unavailable to those who are not mystics within that tradition.

I need to warn you all from the beginning that your instructor has limited competence in many of these things. I do not regard myself as a mystic. I did live as a Benedictine monk for 10 years of my life and in the environment of Benedictine Monasticism for some 15 years. And since I've been married, I have had visions of heaven and hell. But apart from that, I do not bring any particular personal competence to this question apart from that of being a professional student of religion. Nor do I have a total grasp of all the languages that we will be considering. I have sufficient grasp of Hebrew, Greek, Latin, French, and German to control the translations that I use. But most notably, I lack any competence in the important languages for the Islamic tradition, especially Arabic and Persian. I ask your forgiveness from the beginning of the course for any egregious errors in pronunciation.

Let me close this first presentation by talking a little bit about how we're going to move through these lectures. We are going to approach this in fundamentally chronological sequence for each of the traditions in turn, beginning with Judaism, then Christianity, and then Islam. I will try to make you aware, as we move through these units, of the ways in which there are things going on in these other traditions. It is not a simple first Judaism; then, Christianity; and then, Islam, but we have to have some way of organizing the material. This presentation and then two further introductory presentations will try to provide a framework of what I call the "exoteric traditions." What are we talking about when we speak of Judaism, Christianity, and Islam? What are these great families of religion, and what are their similarities and dissimilarities? That will be the next opening lecture. And then I will turn to the biblical basis of mystical symbolism. This is extremely important because the same themes that are found in the biblical narratives are worked and reworked throughout the entire history of mysticism in Judaism and Christianity directly and in Islam indirectly.

The treatment of each tradition, and of mysticism within each tradition, seeks to make clear what is distinctive, as well as what is common. My emphasis is going to be on mystical literature as produced by great masters within the tradition. I will try to let mystics speak for themselves as much as possible. This is a course in which you will be hearing a fair amount of quotations from mystical writers. And it is through the examination of that literature that I will try to pose analytic questions concerning mysticism itself. This is not a course in which I'm setting out to prove that mysticism is real or mysticism is baloney. It is, rather, what have mystics written and what we can learn critically from an examination of that literature.

Although the focus is on the classical sources of the past, each unit will conclude with a lecture on the consideration of the practices of mysticism in Judaism, Christianity, and Islam today. Then the course will end with a set of questions concerning the truth of mystical claims. I'll return to that question "Is it baloney or is there something to it?" and to the question of the viability of mysticism in a very secular world. In short, this course exposes us all to the remarkable visions of reality held by some of the most fascinating writers of our religious past. You will, I think, find them intriguing. The larger question is whether any of us will see them as something more than merely quaint, as possibly even pertinent.

Lecture Two
Family Resemblances and Differences

Scope:

Mysticism is an important facet of the three great monotheistic religions of the West. This lecture provides a necessary framework for placing mysticism within each tradition by a broad introduction to the three traditions in their complex interconnections. In what sense is it appropriate to think of them together as "Western religions"? Considered exoterically as religious systems, what elements do the three religions share, and what features distinguish each of them? Such comparisons help locate the focus of mystical devotion within the respective traditions. Finally, this lecture provides an overview of the role played by each tradition in history, comparing their arcs of growth and influence.

Outline

I. Judaism, Christianity, and Islam are commonly grouped together as "Western religions," a designation that is both inappropriate and appropriate.

    A. Understood geographically or demographically, the characterization is inaccurate.

        1. Today, the West tends to be identified with Europe and the Americas. Although more geographically western in origin than Hinduism or Buddhism, all three religions arose in the Middle East.

        2. All three religions—particularly, Islam and Christianity—have adherents in every part of the world. Judaism retains a family dimension, but the other two traditions transcend ethnicity.

    B. Understood in terms of cultural influence and religious type, the designation "Western religions" has merit.

        1. These three traditions all exercised their first and greatest influence on Western culture, whether as formative or challenging. Medieval European philosophy, for example, is impossible to understand apart from the challenge of Islamic philosophy.

        2. The three Western religions share common family features that distinguish them from the Eastern family

(Hinduism, Taoism, and Buddhism), which likewise share common features.

II. That these three traditions share certain common elements is clear, even though the precise understanding or practice of even these shared elements is subject to variation within each.

    A. Most obviously, they share an understanding of God in relation to the world that is distinct both from the ancient religions out of which they emerged and the great religions of the East.

        1. Judaism, Christianity, and Islam are monotheistic religions: There is but one ultimate power in the world who is the source and goal of everything.

        2. The one God has created the world, which is real but also relative, distinct from God but also dependent on the creator.

        3. This one God who created the world also has a character (intelligence and will) and seeks communication with humans through revelation.

    B. All three traditions are prophetic religions and religions of the book; note, too, that these two notions are connected.

        1. God reveals through creation but also through chosen humans who are prophets: Moses, Jesus, and Muhammad.

        2. Prophets "see" or "hear" in the sights and sounds of ordinary life what they understand as God's word and communicate that word to others.

        3. In each tradition, sacred texts (TaNaK, the Bible, and the Qur'an) contain prophecies that reveal God's word and will for humans.

        4. The prophetic impulse can arise outside the frame of the written word but not in contradiction to it.

    C. The three traditions all recognize the need to interpret the sacred books.

        1. Scriptures have intrinsic complexities, including the use of poetic language, metaphor, allusion, anthropomorphism, and simile, and are characterized by density.

        2. For this reason, sources other than the sacred text must be invoked as a means of interpreting Scripture, including oral Torah, the Holy Spirit, and the Hadith.

3. The religions' interpretations of their sacred books are elaborated into systems of community law: Talmud for Judaism, canon law and theology for Christianity, and Shari'ah for Islam.

D. The three religions all assert that humans are free and agree on the basic form of human response to God.

1. The positive response is obedience, faith, or submission to God's will.

2. The negative response is idolatry, disobedience, apostasy, sin, or *shirking*.

3. Humans express their obedience to God through acts of justice and love toward other humans.

E. All three traditions share a sense that individual and communal life, the world itself, has a future, as well as an end (eschatology).

1. God, the keeper of the book, judges humans on the basis of their deeds.

2. Humans are assigned to a future of bliss or torment on the basis of God's judgment.

3. God also works positively for those who are faithful at the communal level.

F. In each religion, the human response to God is expressed in common forms of piety.

1. Each has set times and seasons of prayer, as well as forms of prayer that share certain features.

2. In each tradition, fasting is valued as a way of expressing the seriousness of one's commitment to God.

3. Each of these traditions has a firm commitment to sharing possessions with others, above all, the poor (almsgiving).

4. Pilgrimage has been a more sporadic practice in Judaism and Christianity but a constant one in Islam.

III. Judaism, Christianity, and Islam also have major points of difference, sometimes within their shared framework.

A. They clearly disagree on which prophet is ultimate, Moses, Jesus, or Muhammad.

B. They have different understandings of revelation through prophetic books.

1. In Judaism and Christianity, human authorship is acknowledged, and Scripture remains sacred even in translation.
2. In Islam, human authorship is denied, and the Qur'an is sacred only in Arabic.

C. The religions assign different levels of authority to sacred texts.
1. Judaism regards neither the New Testament nor the Qur'an as authoritative.
2. Christianity accepts the Old Testament as normative but only as read through the lens of the New Testament; it does not recognize the Qur'an as revelatory.
3. Islam recognizes the Old Testament and New Testament as prophetic books but only as understood within the rewriting of the Qur'an.

D. Messianism (expectation of a Messiah) plays a distinct role in each tradition.
1. In Judaism, Messianism has been a sporadic and not necessarily dominant feature.
2. Christianity is defined by the conviction that Jesus is *the* Messiah.
3. In Islam, Messianism is significant only within Shiism.

E. The traditions place a different emphasis even on shared elements.
1. Law is central to Islam and Judaism in a way that it is not in Christianity.
2. Pilgrimage is important to Islam in a manner not found in Judaism and Christianity.
3. Christianity has a more elaborate system of rituals (sacraments) than Islam or Judaism.

IV. The three religions have had distinct political visions and roles within history.

A. Classical Judaism has been the religion of a diasporic minority since the fall of the Jerusalem Temple in 70 C.E.
1. Jews have had to find a place within an often hostile Gentile majority. Throughout history, Muslims have been far more hospitable to Jews than Christians have been.

    2. The emancipation of the 19th century and the Holocaust of the 20th century threatened the continued existence of Judaism.

    3. The existence of Israel as a Jewish state represents an ambiguous reality for Judaism.

B. Christianity originally had no vision for a larger society but has gone through dramatic political changes.

    1. In the 4th century C.E., Christianity was transformed from the religion of a persecuted minority to the imperial religion.

    2. The vision of "Christendom" meant battle against "infidels," persecution of Jews, and suppression of heretics.

    3. The disestablishment of Christianity (leading to the "post-Constantinian era") creates divisions among Christians concerning the desirability of a "Christian culture."

C. Islam had a definite political vision from the start but has had an inconsistent ability to enact it.

    1. The Shari'ah is not "religious law" so much as a way of structuring all of life in accordance with the will of Allah.

    2. Islam's first great expansion involved military means and political negotiations among states.

    3. After a long period of cultural and political ascendance, Islam went into an age of eclipse.

    4. Reform movements in Islam today argue for the earlier vision: Both individuals and nations must be *islama*, that is, submissive to the will of Allah.

Recommended Reading:

Peters, F. E. *Children of Abraham: Judaism, Christianity, Islam.*

Questions to Consider:

1. Consider the meaning of the terms "exoteric" and "esoteric" and the ways in which they are related to each other in religious traditions.

2. Examine the ways in which "prophecy" is a useful category for perceiving what is common and what is distinctive in these three religious traditions.

Lecture Two—Transcript
Family Resemblances and Differences

This is the second of three preliminary lectures that provide a framework for our consideration of mysticism in Judaism, Christianity, and Islam. In the first, I offered some opening questions and definitions, trying to locate the phenomenon called mysticism in relation to religion and, especially, religious experience. In this lecture, I consider some family resemblances and differences among the three religious traditions. Some of what I say here, as perhaps everything that I said in the first presentation, may be already known to you, but there is some virtue in stating the obvious before moving on to what is more obscure.

To begin with the very obvious, then, Judaism, Christianity, and Islam are commonly grouped together as "Western religions." The designation is both inappropriate and appropriate. If we understand "Western" geographically or demographically, the characterization is inaccurate. Today, the West tends to be identified with Europe and the Americas, and although these three traditions arose geographically more western in origin than Hinduism or Buddhism, all three religions had their foundation in what we now call the Middle East by the measure of full global awareness. And they bear within them a DNA that simply refuses to be equated with what we regard as the West. Demographically, all three religions—above all, Islam and Christianity—have adherents in every part of the world. There are Jewish communities in Africa, Asia, and Latin America. There are Christians in Lebanon, Iraq, and South Korea. There are Muslims in France, in Russia, and Malaysia. And although Judaism retains some elements of family, both Christianity and Islam transcend ethnicity. They are truly world religions demographically. So, geographically and demographically, calling these "Western" religions is inappropriate.

But if we understand the term as cultural influence and religious type, then the designation does have some merit. These three traditions that arose in the Middle East tended to move geographically westward rather than eastward, and they exercised their first and greatest influence on Western culture, whether as formative (as in the case of Judaism and Christianity) or as challenge (as in the case of Islam). Medieval European philosophy, for example, is impossible to understand apart from the challenge that was posed by Islamic philosophy. More important, these three religions share common family features that distinguish them from the Eastern family—Hinduism, Taoism, Buddhism—which likewise share common features. Although the term "Western" is dubious, it is not a mistake to view these three traditions together because of their family resemblance.

Let me begin, then, with some of the obvious common elements that they clearly share, even though the precise understanding or practice of even these shared elements is subject to variation within each. Most obviously, these three religions share an understanding of God in relation to the world that is distinct both from the ancient religions out of which they emerged and the great religions of the East. These are monotheistic religions. Prior to Judaism and Islam, polytheistic religions were the norm in their environment. "Polytheistic" means that the perception of the divine is distributed among many divine persons, sort of an extended family, each member of which is in control of some aspect of reality. Similarly, the Greco-Roman world, out of which earliest Christianity arose, was likewise polytheistic. So each of these traditions claims that there is but one ultimate power in the world, in contrast to a diffusion of divine powers. Perhaps better stated: not that there is one ultimate power in the world, but that there is one ultimate power who is not of the world but who is the source and goal of the world. In monotheistic religions, the divine power is not distributed but concentrated. God is called "holy," which means God is other. God is different than anything that one can see in the empirical realm. In order to approach God, therefore, one has to become also other or holy.

The notion of what "oneness" means, however, in each of these traditions is going to become highly problematic, not least because of the influence of mysticism, but exoterically, all three traditions—Judaism, Christianity, and Islam—are monotheistic religions. There is only one God. Furthermore, this one God has created the world, everything that we see. And the world is real but relative. It is distinct from God but also dependent on the creator and dependent on the creator at every moment, so that God and world are constantly related. In these traditions, creation is not something that happened long ago in the past; creation is an ongoing process by which that which is not comes into being. It is "a process of becoming" that Jews, Christians, and Muslims mean by "creation." Because God created the world real, this means that in each of these traditions, materiality has value. Material things are not despised in themselves as illusory. They are, rather, real; they are simply not ultimate. And because matter is real, body is real, and so is time, because time is body in motion. These traditions affirm the validity of body, of time, and of history. Because these traditions affirm the value of the body and of materiality, this means that each of these traditions struggles with what is particular (that is, grounded in real bodies, real places, real things) and their universal claims. How does one put together what is particular and what is ultimate? We will see that mystics have various ways of trying to deal with that sort of problem.

This one God who created the world also has a character. God is intelligent. God has will. God has a character that is all-powerful. He is a life giver. He is full of mercy and justice, and God is faithful to God's creation. Because God is conceived of not impersonally but personally, all these traditions share the conviction that God seeks to communicate with humans through a process called "revelation." God seeks to be known and understood by humans. And in this respect, the beauty of God's world is both a gift and a bit of a distraction. There is this sense that the beauty of the world can so captivate by its reality that people can grow confused about the difference between creation and the creator and tend to focus upon creation rather than the creator. For this reason, all three traditions are prophetic religions and religions of the book, and these two things go together. God, as I said, reveals through creation, but because humans tend to get confused and distracted by creation, God chooses certain human beings through whom communication in a more direct way can be established with humans. They are called prophets. Moses is a prophet, Jesus is a prophet, and Muhammad is a prophet. Indeed the Qur'an counts 27 prophets before the time of Muhammad, the seal of all the prophets.

Prophets are not people who predict the future. Prophets are people who, rather, speak for God to other humans. They are those who, in the middle of an ordinary conversation, hear an additional word that nobody has actually spoken. They are those who, when viewing exactly the same situation, see a significance that nobody else sees in that situation. The prophet is one who has second sight, second hearing, the capacity to catch the greater significance called God's word in the midst of ordinary human communication and then offers that word of meaning and of challenge to others. In each of these traditions, such prophecies are contained in sacred books. For Jews, it is Torah and, explicitly, the TaNaK, the first five books of Moses; the Neviim, the Prophets; and the Ketuvim, the Writings. These three collections of compositions form the Jewish sacred text. For Christians, it is more or less the same writings as TaNaK, but now called the Old Testament, together with the 27 writings in Greek called the New Testament, to form the Bible. For Muslims, it is the Qur'an, the revelation of Allah to the Prophet Muhammad. All of these contain prophetic words that reveal God's will for humans. So prophets don't predict the future; they reveal God's will to other humans. Now, in principle, in all three religions, the prophetic impulse can arise outside these written texts, outside the written word, although not in contradiction to the written word. And this tension between what is written in Scripture and how prophets act is particularly difficult in the case of Christianity, where the most fundamental revelation of God's word is thought to occur not in a book but in a human person, namely, Jesus of Nazareth.

All three traditions, furthermore, recognize the need to interpret the sacred books. They recognize that the Scriptures have intrinsic difficulties: poetic language, metaphor, allusion, anthropomorphism, density, and simile. They were written long ago for ancient circumstances. How does what was said 2,000 years ago apply today? Scriptures contain contradictions and tensions between one part and another. Religious readers, even mystics, understand that Scriptures bear all of these problems within them, and they recognize, therefore, that other sources than the written text must be invoked as a means of interpreting Scripture. In Judaism, it is the oral Torah, the tradition of the oral interpretation of Scripture. Within Christianity, it is the Holy Spirit. Within Islam, it is the Hadith of the prophet, which we will speak about much more later. The precise role of human intelligence or human reasoning in applying these additional sources to these sacred texts is either implicit or explicit in each tradition. All three of these traditions acknowledge that these interpretations of the sacred books get elaborated into systems of community norms. In Judaism, it is the Talmud. In Christianity, it is a sort of a combination of canon law and theology. In Islam, it is the Shari'ah.

Furthermore, God having revealed God's will to humans in divine books as interpreted within the community, all three of these traditions agree that humans are basically free. This is quite a remarkable conviction, because the freedom of humans to choose for or against God clearly stands in tension with an equally strong conviction that God is all powerful. And we will see that, especially in Islam, the tension between God's power and human freedom becomes acute. But humans are free to respond to God. Their positive response is obedience, or faith, or submission to God's will. The appropriate stance of the creature to the creator is obedience. Love, in the exoteric traditions, is an add-on. The first response to God is not love; it is obedience. It is doing what God wills. What is the negative response? Humans negatively respond through idolatry, disobedience, apostasy, sin, or in Islamic terms, *shirking*—that is, neglect of the divine will.

Finally, all three of these traditions affirm that this human response to God of obedience, of submission, of faith is expressed through acts of justice and love toward other humans. So, corresponding to piety toward God is morality toward the neighbor. All three of these traditions share a sense that individual and communal life, the world itself, has a future. They all have what is called an eschatology, a sense of the end of things. God, the keeper of the book, judges humans on the basis of their deeds. God knows the human heart and cannot be fooled, and so humans individually are assigned a future, either of bliss or of torment, on the basis of God's judgment of who they really are. And the universe for all three of these traditions is more richly populated than among those of us who live in an Enlightenment world. It involves created spirits, good angels, bad angels, or a spirit like the Qur'anic Ibliss, who is capable of making free choices for or against Allah. God also works positively for the people as a whole who are faithful to the Lord. There is a concern for his people, for the children of Abraham, that God will not forsake them, that things will turn out for them communally all right in the long run, that their faith in God is not futile. Eschatology means that just as the world has a definite beginning, so it will have a definite end. These are not religions of the eternal return, of a cyclical sense of time. They are linear. They are teleological. They are moving toward an end.

In each of these traditions, piety toward God is expressed by certain shared forms. Each have set times and seasons of prayer, praying three times a day; praying five times a day; giving a special attention to prayer during the season of the High Holy Days in Judaism, Lent in Christianity, Ramadan in Islam. And they share the forms of prayer—the verbal forms of blessing, of praise, of petitions—and movements during prayer—bowing, prostrating, raising the hands in prayer. All of these are shared among these three great traditions. In each of them, fasting is valued as a way of expressing, through abstention from food, the seriousness of the commitment to God. Robert Feracapine once made the wonderful statement that the "Biblical religions have a sense of feasting and fasting: feast to celebrate the pleasures of life, fasting to celebrate the tragedy of life." Nowhere in the Bible is there any instruction on dieting. Dieting has an entirely different conception of life altogether.

Each of these traditions has a firm commitment to sharing possessions with others, above all, the poor. This is called "almsgiving." It is, in fact, the fundamental requirement of humans in all three of these traditions. They think that as God has blessed and cared for them, so they should care for others. A heedless prosperity is regarded as deeply wrong. A prosperity that neglects the needs of the poor is condemned everywhere in these three traditions.

A final act of piety in all three traditions is the practice of pilgrimage, of seeking a holy place where the divine power might be experienced more profoundly. In ancient Judaism, there were the three great pilgrimage feasts, when people would go to Jerusalem to celebrate. In Christianity, pilgrimage has been fairly sporadic—the attempt to go to Jerusalem or to other holy places: Rome, Canterbury, and other sacred shrines. It is most emphatically required in Islam. The pilgrimage, the Hajj, to Mecca is a requirement of the devout Muslim if it is financially and physically possible to undertake that pilgrimage.

I've scattershot a number of shared features of these three traditions. Judaism, Christianity, and Islam also have major points of difference, often within that shared framework. First, they clearly disagree on which prophet is the ultimate prophet. For Judaism, Moses is the ultimate prophet; Jesus is not a true prophet, and certainly, Muhammad is not recognized as a prophet. In Christianity, Moses is regarded as a prophet, but so is Jesus, the ultimate prophet. Islam generously recognizes both Moses and Jesus as prophets, but it is Muhammad who is the ultimate seal of prophecy.

Each of these traditions has different understandings of revelation through prophetic books. They all have prophecy. They all have sacred books. But the way they view those prophecies in those sacred books is distinct. Here, Judaism and Christianity are alike:

They recognize human authorship of Scripture. Moses wrote Torah. David wrote the Psalms. Solomon wrote Wisdom. The New Testament has the same view. Paul wrote epistles. John, Mark, Luke, and Matthew wrote the four Gospels. Human authorship is acknowledged, and furthermore, Scripture remains sacred even in translation. A Jew is really reading TaNaK in English translation, not simply in Hebrew. A Christian is really reading the Bible when translated and not simply in Hebrew and in Greek. The conception of the holy book in Islam is quite distinct. First, it is not through human authorship. The Qur'an is Allah's direct word, which is heard and repeated by the Prophet Muhammad. And secondly, the Qur'an is sacred only in Arabic, that is, in its original language. If one is reading the Qur'an—as I do—in English translation, I am not strictly reading the Qur'an. I am reading an interpretation of the Qur'an, and it does not have sacred value.

These three traditions ascribe different levels of authority to the sacred texts. Clearly, this follows from the previous point. Judaism regards neither the New Testament nor the Qur'an as authoritative. Christianity accepts the Old Testament—as it calls it—as authoritative but only as read through the lens of the New Testament, and it does not recognize the Qur'an as revelatory. Islam appears to accept both the Old Testament and the New Testament as prophetic books, as it recognizes Moses and Jesus as prophets, but only as understood through the rewriting of those books that is found in the Qur'an. In other words, God delivered holy books both to Jews and to Christians, but as the Qur'an itself says, they messed them up. Jews and Christians sort of messed up the Scriptures, and so the Qur'an gives the final, authoritative version of those Scriptures.

These three traditions disagree about Messianism—that is, the expectation of a Messiah. In Judaism, Messianism has only been a sporadic and not necessarily a dominant feature of the tradition. There are times when Messianism has been a very important feature in Judaism—from the 1st century B.C.E. to the 2nd century C.E., again in the 17th century—but not always. Christianity, in contrast, is totally defined by the conviction that Jesus is the Messiah, so much so that Christians miscategorize Jews as those who are still awaiting the Messiah, a total misrepresentation of what Judaism is about. And in Islam, Messiah is significant only within one sect—that is, the Shi'ah—with the expectation of the Mahdi.

These traditions place a different emphasis even on shared elements. Law is central to Islam and Judaism in a way that it is not in Christianity. Law has always been problematic in Christianity, but in Judaism and Islam, it is essential. Pilgrimage has been important to Islam and even necessary in a way that is less so in Judaism and Christianity. Christianity has a much more elaborate set of rituals at the exoteric level, for example, the seven sacraments, which are not found in Judaism and Islam. Judaism and Islam are much simpler in ritual terms. And I would like to alert you to the very great significance within the mystical tradition of Christian conceptions of the sacrament called the Eucharist, especially the conviction that in the Eucharist, there is a real presence of the body and blood of the risen Lord, Jesus Christ. This is going to be extremely important, especially for medieval Christian mystics.

Finally, all of these traditions have had distinct political visions and roles within history. Although the Law of Moses was written as the law for a society, namely, ancient Israel, classical Judaism has been a diasporic minority. It has been scattered throughout the world in dominant cultures and had to subsist with an intensive separatist identity, shaped around the study of Torah, ever since the fall of the Jerusalem Temple in the year 70 C.E. It has had to try to find a place within an often hostile Gentile majority. And it should be said that throughout history, Muslims have been far more hospitable to Jews than Christians have been. The experience of emancipation by Jews in the 19th century and the experience of the Holocaust in the 20th century have threatened the very existence of Judaism. And Israel is a Jewish state in the present world, but that is a deeply ambiguous reality for religious Jews. Zionism, the effort to return to a Jewish homeland, had as much secular as religious impulse behind it. And today in the State of Israel, there is tension between those who want Israel to be a Jewish state religiously and those who desire it to be a secular state, a place where all Jews can be safe.

Christianity started off with no vision for society. The New Testament is written to small communities scattered throughout the Mediterranean world. The New Testament has no vision for how to order things politically. But Christianity has gone through dramatic political changes. In the 4th century C.E., it went from a persecuted minority to becoming the imperial religion. And Christendom, this strange amalgam of religious and political features, then engaged in centuries-long battles against the "infidels" (Muslims) in the name of

Christ (the Crusades), the persecution of Jews, and the suppression of Christian heretics. The disestablishment of Christianity that came about through political revolutions from the 18th century to the 20th century and led to what is now called the post-Constantinian era creates divisions even today among Christians as to whether or not Christianity should try to go back to Christendom. Should Christianity be pleased at being, like Judaism, a diaspora religion, or should it try to re-create a Christian state?

Islam starts with a definite political vision from the start but has had an inconsistent ability to enact it. The Shari'ah is not religious law so much as a way of structuring all of life in accordance with the will of Allah. And Islam's first great expansion involved military means, as well as political negotiations among states. But after a long period of cultural and political ascendance, when Islam ruled from Spain in the west to India in the east, Islam went into a long period of political decline. And reform movements in Islam today argue for an earlier vision of Islam, not as a religion for the individual but, rather, as a situation in which nations also are *islama*—that is, submissive to the will of Allah.

Lecture Three
The Biblical Roots of Western Mysticism

Scope:

The Hebrew Bible (Old Testament) is the most powerful source both for the premises of Western Mysticism and for its symbolism. Mystics within Judaism, Christianity, and Islam not only read Scripture, but in some sense, they enact it in their lives. This lecture considers the constitutive elements in prophetic religion (a hidden God who can be approached and who approaches; the intersection of the realm of the human and the divine), the powerful examples of mystical experience displayed by the prophets (in particular, Moses, Ezekiel, and Isaiah), and the set of symbols for the human-divine communication presented by such accounts (the pilgrimage, the mount, the cloud, the light, the heavenly throne). In quite a different fashion, the explicitly erotic language of the Song of Solomon provides a way of speaking about human and divine passion.

Outline

I. In this lecture, we turn to the biblical roots of Western Mysticism. It is in the Bible, above all, that the mystic's experience within Judaism, Christianity, and Islam finds a means of expression.

   A. The premises guiding the precritical reading of the Bible (TaNaK, Old Testament) are entirely different from those found among historical critics.
   1. Until the Enlightenment and the rise of historical criticism, the biblical account was read as a faithful report concerning what actually happened in the past.
   2. Study of Scripture was not an exercise of demystification and verification according to critical standards; instead, it was undertaken to gain wisdom concerning the world's past, present, and future.

   B. The biblical portrayal of events and characters is not viewed by religious readers as idealized but as revelatory of real human possibilities.
   1. The construction of the world is as the Bible describes, and characters did what the Bible reports.

2. What the prophets said and did through God's word sets a pattern that others can follow.
3. The Bible is read, above all, as providing a set of examples for its readers.

C. The Hebrew Bible (TaNaK) is a direct source for the patterns and symbols of Jewish and Christian Mysticism and an indirect source for Islam.

II. The figure of the prophet Moses is of fundamental importance because he is the first (and greatest) prophet in TaNaK.

A. The figures preceding Moses also had experiences of God; for example, Adam speaks with God, Abraham hears God, Jacob sees heaven opened, and Joseph interprets dreams.

B. But Moses shows the reader a life that is permeated by the direct experience of God.
1. He encounters God in a burning bush and is commissioned to free his people (Exod. 3:4–14).
2. With the elders, he ascends Mount Sinai and "sees the Lord" (Exod. 24:9–11).
3. He is the Lord's "intimate friend" (Exod. 33:12–15) and learns God's essential attributes (Exod. 34:1–9).
4. He knows the Lord "face to face" (Deut. 34:10–11).

C. The figure of Moses establishes the basic pattern and a considerable amount of symbolism for mystics.
1. The pattern is one of "approaching God" by ascent and pilgrimage, involving a movement from slavery to freedom and demanding purification.
2. The symbols for human access to God include crossing the sea and the desert, ascending the mountain, experiencing a dark cloud and fire, observing a sea of glass or sapphires, and finally, coming to the land of rest.

III. Other prophets in the biblical account expand the repertoire of symbols associated with visions, to some degree, by repeating certain elements.

A. Most significant is the experience of Isaiah, an 8th-century figure who had a vision of God in the Temple and was commissioned as a prophet (Isa. 6:1–13).

1. The Lord appears as enthroned; his "glory" fills the "house" (*hekal* is a palace or mansion); and he is proclaimed as "holy" by angels.
2. The prophet experiences himself as "unclean" but is nevertheless sent to give God's word to the people.

B. Among the exiles, Ezekiel experienced the heavens opening, revealing divine visions (Ezek. 1:4–28), and was also commissioned as a prophet (2:1–4).
1. In his vision, Ezekiel sees the *merkabah*, the heavenly throne-chariot.
2. The *merkabah* is movable and is surrounded by angels, clouds, and flashes of fire. With this vision, Ezekiel knows he is in the presence of God.

C. Also among the exiles (as the pseudonymous composition has it), Daniel is commissioned as a prophet (Dan. 7–12).
1. In the pioneering apocalyptic writing of the book of Daniel, God's plans for the future are disclosed through highly encoded visions.
2. These visions include symbolic numbers and animals and various cosmic elements, all used to communicate a view of history to the prophet. (Dan. 7:9–14).

IV. The Bible is also a rich source of erotic imagery for the mystical understanding of the relationship between God and humans.

A. The prophets speak of the covenant relationship between God and Israel as a marriage.
1. Hoshea (Hos 1–3) pictures the broken and restored covenant in terms of marriage to an unfaithful prostitute who is healed by a return to the desert.
2. Jeremiah uses the same language and introduces the language of "the heart" into the personal relationship with the Lord (Jer. 8:18–23; 20:7–9).
3. Ezekiel tells the story of Israel in terms of a sexual history (Ezek. 16).

B. Most powerful in this respect is the Song of Solomon (Song of Songs), which is erotic poetry centered in the love of a man and woman.
1. The Song of Solomon has no explicit religious motif, and the name of God is not mentioned in it.

2. Yet read against the backdrop of the marriage analogy, it is one of the most important sources for erotic imagery concerning the relationship between the mystic and God.

Recommended Reading:

Heschel, A. *The Prophets*.

Questions to Consider:

1. How do approaches to the Bible that stem from historical criticism differ from the assumptions about the text shared by mystics through the ages?

2. What in the biblical account supports the view of Moses as the first and greatest of the prophets?

Lecture Three—Transcript
The Biblical Roots of Western Mysticism

In describing mysticism as the effort to achieve an unmediated—that is, direct—experience of the divine, I suggested that it cannot avoid mediation in two ways. First, the mystic's experience itself is inevitably shaped by inherited symbols. Second, in order to express an experience to others, shared symbols must be used. In the present lecture, I take up the biblical roots of Western Mysticism. It is in the Bible, above all, that the mystic's experience within Judaism, Christianity, and Islam finds the means of expression. To get into this subject, however, we must remember that the premises guiding precritical reading of the Bible, the TaNaK, or the Old Testament are entirely different from the premises that are found today among historical biblical critics.

Until the rise of the Enlightenment in Europe and the birth of historical criticism in the 18th and 19th centuries, the biblical account was read by religious people as a faithful report of what actually happened in the past. It was true in an obvious and straightforward manner. The study of Scripture was not, as it is among so many contemporary critics, a process of demystification and verification according to critical standards. Historical criticism has proceeded by challenging the historicity of the Creation, the Flood, the Exodus and the conquest, and even of the Davidic kingdom. And more recent critics have challenged the moral standards of Scripture, its views on slavery or women, foreigners, and so forth. All of this was absent by earlier readers of Scripture, for whom the study of the sacred text was undertaken in the pursuit of wisdom concerning the world's past, present, and future. It was read less for information and, rather, more for transformation. This does not mean that the Bible was not read with great care and concentration. Inconsistencies in the sacred text are invariably noted and often give rise to rich interpretations, but the Bible was always read as the inspired and authoritative word of God.

The biblical portrayal of events and characters, then, is not viewed by religious readers as idealized but, rather, as revealing real human possibilities. The construction of the world is as the Bible describes: Heaven and Earth are real; seas can roll back; God can appear on a mountain. And characters do what the Bible describes: Moses strikes the rock and water comes out; the people eat a miraculous manna in the wilderness. Similarly, what the prophets said and did through God's word sets a pattern that others can follow. The prophets reveal the possibilities for others. In effect, what Moses did, the mystic also might be able to do. The Bible, in a word, is read primarily as providing a set of examples that its readers might follow. And the Hebrew Bible, the TaNaK, is the direct source for the patterns and symbols of Jewish and Christian Mysticism and is an indirect source for Islam. Muslims do not read, characteristically, the Bible directly but, rather, through the Qur'anic rewriting of the biblical characters. Nevertheless, it is the same symbolic world shared with Jews and Christians.

I want to look first at the most important prophetic figure, namely, Moses. He is of fundamental importance since he is the first and greatest prophet in TaNaK. Figures preceding Moses in the biblical narrative also had experiences of God. Adam speaks with God. Abraham—the father of all Jews, Christians, and Muslims—hears and obeys God. Hagar, Abraham's female slave and the mother of Ishmael, from whom all Muslims draw their descent, received direct help from God. Jacob sees the heavens opened and angels ascending and descending on a ladder and declares that this is truly the house of God. The young Joseph has powerful dreams, and the older Joseph interprets the dreams of Pharaoh. All of these are in the biblical narrative preceding Moses. But it is the Bible's portrayal of Moses that shows the reader a life that is permeated by the direct experience of God.

When Moses is in exile after he has killed the Egyptian who abused a fellow Israelite, he encounters God in a burning bush. The bush is burning but is not consumed by the fire. Moses is commissioned by God to go to rescue his people. The voice says, "Moses, Moses." And Moses said, "Here am I." Then God said, "Do not come near. Put off your shoes from your feet, for the place on which you are standing is holy ground." And he said, "I am the God of Abraham, the God of Isaac, and the God of Jacob." And Moses hid his face and was afraid of God, this first theophany, this appearance of God. And later in this same incident, Moses asks, "Well, if I go to Egypt and say that the God of Abraham, Isaac, and Jacob has sent me, what else should I say? And they ask me, 'What is his name?'" God said to Moses, "I am who I am." And he said, "Say this to the people of Israel, 'I am has sent me to you.'" This is the first great experience of direct encounter with God by Moses.

Moses does bring the people out of Egypt with a strong hand, with the parting of the Red Sea, in which the waters roll up like a wall on one side and the people of Israel pass through dry-shod. And after "the horses of Pharaoh, with his chariots and his horsemen, went into the sea, the Lord brought back the waters of the sea upon them, but the people of Israel walked through on dry land in the midst of the sea. Then Miriam, the prophetess, the sister of Aaron, took a timbrel in her hand; and all the women went out with timbrels and dancing." I'm choosing this text because of the prophets dancing and singing, which we will see later in the tradition. "And Miriam sang to them, 'Sing to the Lord for He has triumphed gloriously / The horse and his rider, he has thrown into the sea.'"

Moses brings the people to Mount Sinai, and the Lord comes down on the mountain in a great cloud of smoke and burning on the mountain. And the people grow afraid to approach the mountain, even though Moses tells them, you must prepare yourself for this encounter with the Lord. You need to wash your garments. And he said to the people, "Be ready by the third day. Do not go near a woman." The reason I read that text is because it will begin to give us a sense of sexual aestheticism as an element of preparation for a mystical encounter with God. And Moses then goes up into the mountain. Because the people are afraid, they say, you go up. We're too afraid. And Moses goes up and draws nearer to the thick darkness where God is. The ascent of the mountain is an ascent into darkness. This is going to be an extraordinarily important image for the mystical experience as we read into this tradition.

At a later point in the story, there is a very short and quite remarkable account. This is in chapter 24 of Exodus. And in its entirety, it says:

> Then Moses and Aaron, Nadab and Abi'hu and seventy of the elders of Israel went up, and they saw the God of Israel, and there was under his feet as it were a pavement of sapphire stone, like the very heaven for clearness. And he did not lay his hand on the chief men of the people of Israel; they beheld God, and ate and drank.

This is a strange and fascinating account of human access to God on the mountain, but please note that image of the sapphire floor, the sapphire sea upon which God stands.

Moses is God's intimate in this story. In Exodus 33, it says, "The Lord used to speak to Moses face to face, as a man speaks to his friend." So intimate are they that Moses asks, can I see your face? This is one of the oddities of the biblical account, because we just read a story in which Moses and the elders went up and saw God, but in this story in chapters 33 and 34 of Exodus, God says to Moses, you can't see my face. Nobody can see God and live, but if you situate yourself in a cleft of this mountain, I will pass by, and you can see the back of me.

> And the Lord descended in the cloud and stood with him there. … The Lord passed before him, and proclaimed, "The Lord, the Lord, a God merciful and gracious, slow to anger, and abounding in steadfast love and faithfulness."

So Moses has this encounter with God on the mountain, not face to face but only seeing the backside of God, and God reveals his essential characteristics of faithfulness and loving kindness toward the people. Moses is the first and the greatest of the prophets.

The book of Deuteronomy, which is the final book of Torah (the five books of Moses), concludes in chapter 34:10–11 with this encomiastic account of Moses:

> There has not arisen a prophet since in Israel like Moses, whom the Lord knew face to face, none like him for all the signs and wonders which the Lord sent him to do in the land of Egypt, to Pharaoh and to all his servants and to all his land and for all the mighty power and all the great and terrible deeds which Moses wrought in the sight of all Israel.

There are two aspects of this passage that I want to point out. The first is, again, the repetition that Moses saw God face to face. What is a prophet? A prophet is a mystic, somebody who has this direct vision of God. Secondly, because Moses saw God face to face, he was able to do these powerful, miraculous deeds. We will see repeatedly in these traditions how visions of God and miraculous deeds go hand in hand with regard to mystics.

The figure of Moses establishes the basic pattern and a considerable amount of symbolism for mystics in the tradition. The pattern is one of approaching God by ascent and by movement of pilgrimage. These are spatial metaphors for something that is happening internally. One goes up on a mountain into the cloud, seeing God.

One moves on pilgrimage from the slavery of Egypt into the freedom of the Promised Land. This is a movement that enables one to come to the place where God wants people to be. We saw in the image of the people at the foot of the mountain that they had to become holy; they had to prepare themselves in order to encounter God. The symbols of human access to God include the crossing of the sea and the desert; of ascending the mountain; of experiencing a dark cloud and fire, a sea of glass, or a sea of sapphires, and the land of rest. All of these symbols will recur in later mystical traditions. Put them in your glossary and keep them handy for when we continue.

I want to turn now to other prophets in the biblical account who expand the repertoire of symbols associated with visions. But they expand this repertoire, to some degree, by repeating elements over and over again. Most significant is the vision of Isaiah the prophet. Isaiah is an 8th-century prophet. In chapter 6 of Isaiah, we have the prophet experiencing a vision of God in the Temple and his commissioning as a prophet. The Lord appears as enthroned. His glory, his presence, fills the house, and he is proclaimed as holy by angels. In your outline, I make a point of the fact that the house here is called a *hekal*. The word is more technically a palace, a mansion; it is a huge house. We will see the importance of this term in later Jewish Mysticism when mystics go into the palace of God. Let me read this passage:

> In the year that King Uzzi'ah died I saw [it's a vision] the Lord sitting upon a throne [so if God is king, then God sits upon the throne], high and lifted up; and his train filled the temple. Above him stood the seraphim [these are angels]; each had six wings: with two he covered his face, with two he covered his feet, and with two he flew. And one called to the other and said: "Holy, holy, holy is the Lord of hosts; the whole earth is full of his glory."

So God's holiness here is such that the prophet Isaiah cries out, "Woe is me! For I am lost; for I am man of unclean lips, and I dwell in the midst of a people of unclean lips; for my eyes have seen the King of hosts." So [God] touches [Isaiah's] mouth and says—he takes one of the seraphim, grabs a torch, and touches the lips of the prophet and he says:

> "Behold, this has touched your lips; your guilt is taken away, and your sin forgiven." And I heard the voice of the Lord

saying, "Whom shall I send, and who will go for me?" Then I said, "Here am I! Send me."

So this vision of the Lord in the Temple with the angels, with the glory, with the cloud, all of this commissions the prophet to go to the people with the words of the Lord.

This image is of a throne inside a palace. Let's look at another prophet, namely, Ezekiel, who is with the exiles in Babylon, and he experiences, in the very beginning of the book of Ezekiel, the heavens opening and the giving to him of a commission as a prophet. The vision of Ezekiel is extraordinarily complex but also extraordinarily important, because this vision of Ezekiel is going to be at the heart of Jewish Mysticism for centuries. Ezekiel sees the heavens open. He sees a stormy wind come out of the north and then flashes of fire coming out of the darkness, and out of the midst of those flashing flames is an appearance of four living creatures, each with four faces and four wings. And they're hovering about and moving in the midst of that fire-filled cloud, with the wings touching one another and so forth. But here's where it gets very, very interesting. As each of these spirits moved about in the midst of the living creatures, there was something that looked like burning coals of fire, like torches moving to and fro among the living creatures.

> and the fire was bright, and out of the fire went forth lightning. And the living creatures darted to and fro, like a flash of lightning. Now as I looked at the living creatures, I saw a wheel upon the earth beside the living creatures, one for each of the four of them … [and it was] like the gleaming of a crysolite … and their construction being as it were a wheel within a wheel.

What is Ezekiel seeing? What he is seeing comes to be called, in the tradition, the *merkabah*, the heavenly throne-chariot. Here is a vision of God on a throne, and the throne has wheels. It's movable, and it is surrounded by angels, and clouds, and flashes of fire, and so forth. And Ezekiel then knows that he is in the presence of God the king. Later Jewish Mysticism is going to put together the palace, the throne, and the throne-chariot as symbols for access to the presence of God.

Also among the exiles is the prophet Daniel, and his vision occurs in the first of the works that are called apocalyptic writings.

"Apocalyptic" means "unveiling." By its very nature, this literature communicates that it is unveiling secrets that are available to the prophet or to the seer but not available to others. It is revealing hidden realities, and as so often happens in this literature, the writing is pseudonymous. The actual Daniel is in the time of the Babylonian exile, but the book of Daniel is written around the year 170 B.C.E. The prophet Daniel has a series of dream-visions, and in this pioneering apocalyptic writing, God's plans for the future are disclosed through highly encoded visions. Here is where we begin to get visions of the future. Of course, it's an effective future, since it's actually talking about the present since it is a pseudonymous work.) Visions include highly symbolic numbers—3, 7, 12, and so forth—symbolic animals, and various cosmic elements—the Sun, the Moon, the stars, the planets, the sea, the Earth. All of these are involved in very elaborate visions that seek to communicate a view of history to the prophet. Daniel says, "As I looked, thrones were placed [again, the thrones] and one that was ancient of days took his seat; his raiment was white as snow, and the hair of his head like pure wool; his throne was fiery flames, its wheels were burning fire."

So you see now the heavenly throne-chariot, the *merkabah*, again recurs in this vision of Daniel, which is centuries after the time of Ezekiel. Clearly, there is literary dependence going on here, the vision of one prophet provides the symbols for the vision of another prophet.

> And I saw in the night visions, and behold, with the clouds of heaven there came one like a son of man, and he came to the Ancient of Days and was presented before him. And to him was given dominion and glory and kingdom, that all peoples, nations, and languages should serve him; his dominion is an everlasting dominion, which shall not pass away, and his kingdom one that shall not be destroyed.

This is a message of hope for the people of Israel, "one like a son of man." Later Christians will read this vision of Daniel, and they will discover in that son of man to whom God gives dominion, Jesus, the resurrected man from Galilee. This vision will have great influence on later Jewish Mysticism.

Up to this point, we've looked at some of the basic pattern of Jewish Mysticism, which is one of ascent and of pilgrimage, and we have seen the accumulation of certain visionary symbols: the symbol of cloud, the symbol of the shining floor which is either made of glass, or sapphires, or crysolite, or gleaming bronze. We've seen the symbol of the palace, the throne room, and the heavenly throne-chariot. All of these will recur over and over again in the Jewish and, to some extent, Christian mystical tradition.

The Bible is also a rich source of erotic imagery for the mystical understanding of the relationship between God and humans. This is another dimension of mysticism—not the knowledge dimension or visionary dimension but the affective dimension. The Bible pictures the relationship between God and Israel as analogous to the relationship between a husband and wife, so that the covenant of marriage between husband and wife corresponds to the covenant between God and the people. It was a natural step for prophets like Hoshea to picture the broken and restored covenant between God and Israel in terms of the prophet's marriage to a prostitute who has gone after other lovers and her restoration by a return to the desert— that is, the place of intimacy where Israel experienced God directly. The prophet Jeremiah uses the same sort of language and, furthermore, introduces the language of the heart into this prophetic experience.

> The wound of the daughter of my people is my heart wounded, I mourn, and dismay has taken hold on me. Is there no balm in Gilead? Is there no physician there? Why then has the health of the daughter of my people not been restored?

Again, Jeremiah cries out to the Lord:

> Oh Lord, thou hast deceived me, and I was deceived. …

> "I will not mention him or speak any more in his name," but there is in my heart as it were a burning fire shut up in my bones, and I am weary with holding it in, and I cannot.

Similarly, the prophet Ezekiel has a powerful vision of the relationship between God and Israel, the whole history of God and Israel, in terms of a very tangled sexual history, wherein God finds Israel as a very young child, and marries her, and then makes her his wife, and then she betrays him.

> When I passed by you again and looked upon you, behold, you were at the age for love; and I spread my skirt over you,

and covered your nakedness [there is sexual intercourse]: yea, I plighted my troth to you and entered into a covenant with you, says the Lord God, and you became mine.

And then the passage goes on to describe how God bathed her with water, and washed off her blood, and anointed her with oil, and clothed her splendidly, and gave her riches, and made her famous throughout the world as the wife of the Lord. "But you trusted in your beauty and played the harlot because of your renown and lavished your harlotries on any passerby." This is very powerful, the language of eroticism to express the relationship between God and humans. It is also extraordinarily dangerous language, because as it turns out, God's punishment of the people of Israel, imaged as the punishment of a bride, can easily be read by literalists as an excuse for spousal abuse, which it was not intended to be. But you see how mystics would take such language of eroticism, of sexual intercourse, of attraction between lovers, as signifying something of the powerful affective dimension of the quest for God.

Most powerful in this respect is the Song of Songs, otherwise known as the Song of Solomon, which occurs among the writings of the Old Testament. It is powerful, erotic poetry, centered in the love of a man and a woman. They are not, apparently, married. It has no explicit religious motif; the name of God is not mentioned in this book, which is one of the reasons why it was difficult to include it in the Bible. Yet read against the backdrop of that analogy between God and Israel as being married partners, the Song of Songs becomes one of the most important sources for erotic imagery concerning the relationship between the mystic and God.

The Song of Songs begins, "Oh that you would kiss me with the kisses of your mouth!" We will see how Bernard of Clairvaux devotes four sermons to that one line.

> Oh that you would kiss me with the kisses of your mouth! For your love is better than wine, your anointing oils are fragrant, your name is oil poured out; therefore, the maidens love you. Draw me after you, let us make haste. The king has [drawn] me into his chambers. We will exult and rejoice in you, we will extol your love more than wine; rightly do they love you. [The king] brought me to the banqueting house, and his manner over me was love. Sustain me with raisins, refresh me with apples; for I am sick with love. O that his

left hand were under my head and that his right hand embraced me! I adjure you, O daughters of Jerusalem, by the gazelles or the hinds of the field, that you stir not up nor awaken love until it please.

We find in these visions and in this erotic language a basic set of symbols that mystics will work and rework throughout the entire traditions in Judaism, Christianity, and Islam.

Lecture Four
Mysticism in Early Judaism

Scope:

During the Hellenistic period (c. 300 B.C.E.–200 C.E.), Judaism had not yet reached its eventual normative form, and Jews both in Palestine and in the Diaspora displayed a variety of ways of maintaining fidelity to the covenant while negotiating with the prevailing cultural influence of Greece and the political dominance of Rome. It is possible to detect three forms of mystical expression among Jews in this period. The first is found in apocalyptic literature, particularly in its emphasis on the ascent of the seer to heaven. The second occurs among the Essenes, the sectarian community at Qumran, where the form of community and forms of worship and writing all point to a mystical sensibility. The third is found among Hellenistic Jews, such as Philo of Alexandria, who interpret Scripture allegorically and conceive of Judaism in terms of a mystery.

Outline

I. With this lecture, we begin consideration of mysticism in each of the three great monotheistic religions of the West.

   A. For each of these units, it is important to remember that a great deal more mystical experience was going on than was written about, and a great deal more was written about than we're able to deal with.

   B. Mystics know their precedents well, but critical scholars have been slower to connect all the dots into a coherent historical picture.

II. Judaism has roots in the biblical religion of ancient Israel but took its classical shape between roughly 350 B.C.E. and 200 C.E. Jews sought to define their religious and cultural identity in a context of conflict and division: How could they best observe Torah and obey God?

   A. Jews in Palestine—newly committed to the covenant with the Lord and dedicated to Torah as the law of the land— contended with the challenge of Greco-Roman culture and rule.

1. Hellenism had been in Palestine since Alexander the Great (d. 323 B.C.E.) and offered a sophisticated culture and a more tolerant, polytheistic religion.
2. Rome had made Palestine a part of the empire under Pompey in 63 B.C.E. and governed through prefects, challenging Jewish sovereignty.
3. Some Jews thought assimilation possible, while others who had political, as well as religious, convictions divided into sects.
4. Jews who violently resisted foreign influence helped generate the war against Rome that ended with the destruction of the temple in 70 C.E.

B. Jews in the Diaspora—more than twice as many as lived in Palestine—were more directly affected by the dominant culture.
1. Already by the year 250 B.C.E., they had translated the Hebrew Bible into Greek (the Septuagint) and used Hellenistic modes of interpretation.
2. Their religious devotion was that of an intentional community; loyalty to God was not identified with specific political and social institutions.

C. Literary evidence points to a powerful religious spirit among Jews of the time, whether in Palestine or in the Diaspora.
1. In Palestine, crowds made the pilgrimage to Jerusalem and gathered at great feasts, such as the Passover.
2. In Palestine and in the Diaspora, synagogues were centers for the study of Torah and prayer.

III. In Palestinian Judaism, at least two manifestations of mysticism appear during this period of turmoil.

A. Apocalyptic literature, such as the book of Daniel, gives us a view of history according to which God is in charge, will intervene, and will save his people so that they will be triumphant in the future. The religious message is that adherents must endure and God will prove faithful to the people.
1. Among the earliest apocalyptic writings is *I Enoch*, ascribed to an ancient hero. Originally composed in Hebrew or Aramaic, it is extant in Ethiopic, and Aramaic fragments have been found at Qumran.

2. It is an extraordinarily complex work, but at its heart are a series of visions experienced by Enoch. In the first of these (*I Enoch* 14:8–25), we find many elements drawn from the prophetic visions in the Bible.

3. Why were such works written? To teach, comfort, exhort? Do they report actual experiences or imagine them? It is even possible that they were written as a means to induce mystical experience.

B. The sectarian community of Essenes at Qumran reveals a Jewish commitment to God that anticipates many later features of Monasticism: a community separate from the world, living a common life that was dedicated to study and prayer, following a strict rule, and practicing rituals of purity.

1. An intense personal piety is shown by the hymns (*Hodayoth*), possibly composed by the Teacher of Righteousness, the community's founder.

2. In *Hodayoth* 5, the Teacher of Righteousness is well aware of his loneliness before God, yet he retains the hope of standing among the holy ones.

3. The *Songs of Sabbath Sacrifice* portrays community worship as participating in that of the angels.

4. The vision of the Qumran community of itself as a replacement temple is a mystical construal of reality.

IV. In the Diaspora, Philo of Alexandria, who read the Greek version of Scripture in the Septuagint in the style of Greek philosophers, had a thoroughly Platonic understanding of the world—he made Plato's distinction between the phenomenal and the noumenal.

A. How representative was Philo's form of mysticism, what we might call biblical Platonism?

1. An exaggerated position argues that Hellenistic Judaism was a mystical version of Judaism in contrast to that found in Palestine.

2. Some say that Philo's view is completely anomalous, that there weren't any Jews who read Scripture as he did.

3. But some evidence, such as the writings of Pseudo-Orpheus, suggests that Philo was not alone.

B. Three points in particular point to Philo's mystical tendencies.

1. He describes Moses in terms of a mystical ascent that can be followed by others (*Life of Moses* 1.158–159).
2. He speaks of his own life in terms that strongly suggest a mystical path (*On the Creation* 71; *On the Special Laws* 3.6).
3. Philo also speaks in glowing terms of Jewish monks, both in Palestine (probably the Essenes) and some local Jews in Egypt, whom he calls the Therapeutae (*Every Good Man is Free*; *Hypothetica*; *On the Contemplative Life*).
4. What we see in Philo, the seeking in the text of Torah deeper meanings that can reveal realities about God, will be much more in evidence in the future of Jewish Mysticism.

Recommended Reading:

Goodenough, E. R. *By Light, Light: The Mystic Gospel of Hellenistic Judaism*.

Questions to Consider:

1. Discuss the ways that mystical literature appropriates and reconfigures symbols learned from earlier compositions.
2. Consider the possible relationships between the "experience" of mysticism and its "literary" expression.

Lecture Four—Transcript
Mysticism in Early Judaism

With this presentation, we begin consideration of mysticism in each of the three great monotheistic religions of the West, beginning with Judaism. For each of these units, it's good to begin with several realizations. The first is that even though we are highly selective in our choice of mystical literature that we will be considering, it's important to remember that a great deal more mystical experience was going on than was written about, and a great deal more was written about than we're able to deal with. The second realization is that although mystics in each tradition have been well aware of their own history—they know their precedents very well—critical scholars, scholars of religion, such as we are in this course, have been slower to connect all the dots into a coherent picture. The scholarly history of Jewish Mysticism, for example, is a work still very much in progress.

Beginning with mysticism in earliest Judaism, it is necessary above all to make the simple point that Judaism as a religion is not the same as the religion of ancient Israel that we read about in the Bible. It has roots in biblical religion but took its classical shape between roughly 350 B.C.E. and 200 C.E. Jews living during that epoch were forced to define their religious and cultural identity in a context of conflict and division. How could they best observe Torah? How could they best obey God's Commandments when faced with severe cultural displacement? Jews in Palestine had freshly returned from the exile filled with zeal for God's place, for his land, for his Law. They were newly committed to the covenant with the Lord, and they were dedicated to the observance of Torah. But they had to contend with the challenge of an aggressive Greco-Roman culture. Hellenism, Greek culture, had been in Palestine since the time of Alexander the Great, who died in the year 323 B.C.E. Greeks had established Greek cities throughout Palestine and offered a sophisticated culture based in the Greek language, rather than in Hebrew, and they offered a more tolerant, open, polytheistic religious system, in contrast to the cramped narrowness of Jewish Monotheism. Jews were invited to pool their God in with the great synchronistic system of Hellenistic Polytheism. After the death of Alexander, when Palestine had become a pawn between rival Greek empires, Rome moved in. Rome intervened in the person of Pompey in the year 63 B.C.E., brought

Palestine into the vast Roman Empire, and governed that province through a series of military prefects, thus annihilating any Jewish pretensions to sovereignty over its own land.

Faced with the challenges of Greek culture and Roman rule, some Jews in Palestine thought it was perfectly possible to assimilate, to get along by going along and remaining Jewish while adapting these ways. But others divided themselves into various sects that had both political and religious convictions. So the characters we read about in the Gospels, the Pharisees and the Sadducees, represented quite distinct political positions. The Pharisees were internally removed from the political sphere but tried to maintain a separate identity. The Sadducees went along by going along and were much more welcoming of Hellenistic culture and Roman rule. The Essenes, whom we will talk about a bit later in this presentation—and who do not appear, by the way, in the New Testament—took a more stringent view, and they withdrew from society altogether to establish a separate, quasi-monastic existence in the wilderness of Judaea. There were even some, like the Zealots, who entered into violent resistance of Roman rule and, over the course of the 1st century, built toward the great war with Rome that lasted between the years 67 and 70 and led to the destruction of the Temple, one of the pivotal dates in the history of Judaism. And they still were not totally suppressed by Roman rule and continued outbreaks of resistance, climaxing in the Bar Kochba Revolt, which ended in the year 135 with the virtual destruction of the city of Jerusalem and its renaming so that, at that point, Palestinian Judaism fundamentally was an entirely different posture. In short, Jews in Palestine were threatened from without and divided from within in terms of their religious and political responses.

Most Jews during this period, however, did not live in Palestine. By far, the greatest number of Jews—over twice as many Jews as lived in Palestine—lived in what was called the Diaspora, that is, the scattering of Jews throughout the Mediterranean world living in Jewish communities within the great urban centers of the Greco-Roman world. They were even more directly affected by the dominant Greco-Roman culture. Already by the year 250 B.C.E., they had translated the Hebrew Bible into Greek; it was called the Septuagint. And they read that Greek Bible in very much the same way that Greeks read their sacred texts. They applied allegorical interpretation to the books of Moses in the same way that Stoic philosophers applied allegorical interpretation to the Homeric myths. Why? Because those myths had scandalous and deeply problematic aspects to them, and allegory was a philosophical way of reading sacred texts in order to save the texts and save the traditions. Hellenistic Jews in the Diaspora read their version of the Bible in exactly the same way, so actually, Jews in the Diaspora were better off in some respects, because their religious devotion to God was that of an intentional community. They could gather around the synagogue. Their loyalty to God was not identified with specific political and social institutions. Jews in Palestine didn't have that choice; to be a Jew in Palestine meant either that you have a temple or you don't have a temple. Either the land is holy or isn't holy. You have a Jewish king or you don't have a Jewish king. For Jews in the Diaspora, it was perfectly possible to go to the gymnasium, learn Homer, and then go to the synagogue and read Torah. Both had very little political ramifications.

Whether in Palestine or in the Diaspora—the two great places, Hebrew-speaking, Greek-speaking (although Greek was spoken throughout the entire world)—the literary evidence suggests that Judaism was a powerful and powerfully alive religious movement in these centuries. Judaism was lively. It was growing. It was attractive to outsiders. It was gaining rather than losing adherents in these centuries. In Palestine, the evidence shows us hundreds of thousands, perhaps even a million people gathering at great feasts, like the Passover, in the environs of Jerusalem to celebrate the great pilgrimage feasts. In Palestine and in Diaspora, synagogues were lively centers for the study of Torah and prayer. So the elements of mysticism that I will begin talking about now arise out of what is very clearly a fervent, deeply committed—if also deeply divided and conflicted—Judaism of the centuries between 350 B.C.E. and 200 C.E.

I would like to look first at mysticism or evidence for mysticism in Palestine. We have at least two indications of Jewish Mysticism appearing during this period of turmoil. The first appears in apocalyptic literature. I've already defined, in an earlier presentation, the term "apocalyptic," when I spoke about the book of Daniel, which is really the first full work that appears in this particular genre. I noted there that it is pseudonymous in authorship, as virtually all apocalyptic literature is. It has visions in which Daniel saw night visions and dreams of various things. These visions have a dense symbolism of numbers, cosmic elements, animals, and so forth. And within all of this symbolism, there is a view of history which is simply this: Appearances to the contrary, God is in charge, and although history seems to be going to hell in a hand basket, God will intervene and save God's people so that those who are now oppressed will in the future prove triumphant. And the religious message of apocalyptic [literature] is quite simple: Hold on, endure; God will prove faithful to the people.

Among the very earliest apocalyptic writings we have is a work called *I Enoch*. Now, *I Enoch* is typical because it ascribes a contemporary work to an ancient hero. In this case, Enoch, who appears in the fifth chapter of Genesis, was ancient indeed, but he possibly was still around, because Genesis mysteriously says Enoch walked with God and was seen no more, which could be taken to mean that Enoch had access to the presence of God. So he was the perfect hero to represent visionary ascents into the presence of God. The *First Book of Enoch* was originally composed in Hebrew or Aramaic, but it is extant in Ethiopic, and certain Aramaic fragments have been found among the Dead Sea Scrolls at Qumran, this library at Qumran that was uncovered in the year 1947.

I Enoch is, by anybody's account, an extraordinarily complex literary work. It is—let's face it—incomprehensible as a literary work, but at its heart are a series of visions that are experienced by Enoch. In the first of these, which I will now read, we find many elements drawn from the prophetic visions that we have learned about from our survey of the biblical literature. This is *I Enoch* 14:8 following:

> And behold I saw the clouds. And they were calling me to a vision; and the fogs were calling me; and the course of the stars and the lightnings were rushing me and causing me to desire; and in the vision, the winds were causing me to fly and rushing me up high into heaven. And I kept coming into heaven, until I approached a wall that was built of white marble … and the inner walls were like mosaics of white marble [that's that floor again], the floor of crystal, the ceiling like the path of the stars and lightnings between which stood fiery cherubim [the angels again] and their heaven of water; and flaming fire surrounded the walls and its gates were burning with fire and I entered into the house.

The word here is that Hebrew word *hekal*, which I first spoke about when describing the vision of Isaiah. Enoch enters into a heavenly palace. He continues a bit further on:

> As for its floor, it was of fire and it was lightning and the path of the stars; and as for the ceiling, it was flaming fire. And I observed and saw inside it a lofty throne—its appearance was like crystal, and its wheels like the shining sun.

You hear the crystal, see the throne, the wheels; this is the *merkabah*. This is the symbol for the presence of God.

> It was difficult to look at it. And the Great Glory was sitting upon it—as for his gown, which was shining more brightly than the sun, it was whiter than any snow. None of the angels was able to come in and see the face of the Excellent and the Glorious One; and no one of the flesh can see him— the flaming fire was round about him.

So this is an astounding vision of the presence of God in the third heaven, to which Enoch ascends to enter into God's presence.

> And the Lord called to me with his own mouth and said to me, "Come nearer to me, Enoch, and to my holy Word." And he lifted me up and brought me near to the gate, but I continued to look down with my face.

This is an extraordinary vision written by a Jew in Palestine in the first two centuries B.C.E.

The question is: Why were works like this written? Why the visions? Were they written to teach, to comfort, to exhort? I think the answer to each of those is yes. But a harder question is: Do they report actual experiences, or do they imagine them? And then here we come to a place where criticism really finds it very difficult to enter. Because of the possibility that I mentioned earlier, it is possible that they were written as a means to induce experience. Throughout all of our study of mystical literature, we will find that it is impossible to make a hard and fast distinction between the literary and the experiential because of the way in which those two dimensions go together. I may have an experience and clothe it in these symbols that are highly imaginary. You may read that symbolic rendering and have the experience. I may write another vision in order to have a similar kind of experience. The whole process of literature and mystical experience, which is suggested by the production of literature like *I Enoch*, remains very complex and difficult to determine.

Let's look at second example of Palestinian Mysticism. I mentioned the Dead Sea Scrolls that were found at Qumran in 1947, and these introduce us to a sectarian community of Jews, usually identified with Essenes, who lived out their commitment to God—their commitment to Torah—in a way that anticipates many dimensions of later Christian Monasticism. They are a community separate from the world. They flee society and form their own community. Some of them, at least, were celibate. They shared their possessions in common; nobody called anything they had their own, but they lived by a common life. They dedicated their days to study and prayer, and they followed a strict rule of life and had such things as excommunication for not obeying the rules. They practiced strict rules of ritual purity. They were, in their own eyes and in ours, really intense Jews. They were far more committed to the strict observance to Torah than those other Jews who continued to associate either with the heathen or (almost as bad) to associate with other Jews who associated with the heathen, which was pretty much the position of the Pharisees.

The library which we discovered, mostly in fragmentary form, at Qumran displays a remarkable range of compositions—sectarian compositions, interpretations of Torah, and liturgical compositions. Among the most fascinating of the compositions come from the Teacher of Righteousness, who was, in all likelihood, the founder of the community, and he wrote a series of *Hodayoth*, or hymns, which reflect a deep personal piety and devotion to God but remarkably without any visionary element at all. We read, for example, from *Hodayoth* 5:

> I thank Thee, O Lord for thou hast redeemed my soul from the Pit, and from the Hell of Abaddon. Thou hast raised me up to everlasting height. I walk on limitless level ground and I know that there is hope for him whom Thou hast shaped from dust for the everlasting Council. Thou hast cleansed a perverse spirit of great sin that it may stand with the host of the Holy Ones, and that it may enter [into] the community with the congregation of the Sons of Heaven. …

> And yet I, a creature of clay, what am I? Kneaded with water, what is my worth and my might?

This is quite different than Enoch. The Teacher of Righteousness doesn't go up into a heavenly palace but is well aware of his loneliness before God, and yet there is this hope of standing among the holy ones. And when we turn to some of the liturgical compositions, the compositions that seem to suggest worship at Qumran, we see the remarkable character of some writings that are called the *Songs of the Sabbath Sacrifice*, which portray community worship as participating in the heavenly worship of the angels.

This is a common theme that we will discover in mysticism: that the participation in lonely human rituals actually is a form of participation in what is also happening in the sphere of the divine. And so the Qumran liturgical fragment suggests that the members of a community who are gathered together in prayer and offering spiritual sacrifices to God are actually participating in the angelic worship of God in heaven. It is a mysticism of a sort. It's certainly a mystical construal of reality, because the Qumran community envisaged itself as a replacement temple. The Temple in Jerusalem, the physical temple, they said, is hopelessly corrupt. The priesthood is corrupt. The sacrifices are lawless. We are God's spiritual temple in the desert. Notice here exoteric, esoteric: the outward ritual of the temple, but here in the wilderness, where all we do is sit, and study, and say words of prayer, and meditate, we are the true inner spiritual sacrifices being offered to God. And so it's logical that they should think of themselves as already participating in the angelic worship that is taking place in heaven.

But we don't have any visions. Well, maybe. There is the tiny fragment found at Qumran which describes—you're not going to be surprised—the divine throne-chariot, the *merkabah*. It's a tiny fragment, but it suggests that there was some form of speculation of this sort going on in that community. The passage reads:

> The Cherubim bless the image of the Throne-Chariot above the firmament, and they praise the majesty of the fiery firmament beneath the seat of His Glory. And between the turning wheels, Angels of Holiness come and go, as it were a fiery vision of most holy spirits.

So the vision of Ezekiel is contemporized and brought to bear on their own prayer experience as one which brings them into the presence of God.

Very briefly, I would like to look at the mysticism found in a Diaspora figure, Philo of Alexandria. He read the Greek version of Scripture in the Septuagint, and he read it allegorically in the style of Greek philosophers. Philo had a thoroughly Platonic understanding of the world—that is, he made Plato's distinction between the phenomenal (that which can be seen, and touched, and so forth, and tasted and smelled) and the noumenal (that which was really real, the world of forms). When Philo read his Bible and saw Earth and heaven, he read it in Platonic terms as the phenomenal and the noumenal. Heaven is where God is, and that's what's most real; Earth is where we are, and that's less real than where God is. With that combination of what might be called biblical Platonism, Philo shapes a distinctive form of mysticism. The critical question with regard to Philo is: How representative was he of Hellenistic Jews? An exaggerated position argues that all of Hellenistic Judaism, with Philo as its prime representative, was a sort of mystical version of Judaism in contrast to that found in Palestine. At an opposite extreme, some say that Philo is completely isolated and anomalous and that there weren't any Jews like him. A better position, especially based on evidence of other writing, such as a poet called Pseudo-Orpheus, suggests that Philo represents a larger segment of the Jewish population in the Diaspora, although he certainly was far more prolific in literary composition than the others were.

Three points in particular point to Philo's mystical tendencies. First, he refers to Moses in terms of a mystical ascent that can be followed by others. "Moses was named god and king of the whole nation and entered, we are told into the darkness where God was [notice how he chokes this], that is, into the unseen, invisible, incorporeal, and archetypal essence of existing things." Philo reads the climb into the cloud and the mountain as a transition from the phenomenal into the noumenal, and thus, he goes on to say Moses becomes an example of what we can do. So he describes Moses in terms of a mystical ascent.

He also speaks of his own life in terms that strongly suggest that he himself was a mystic. He says sometimes his mind is:

> seized by a sober intoxication, like those filled with Corybantic frenzy, and is inspired, possessed with a longing

far other than theirs and a nobler desire. Wafted by this to the topnotch ark of the things perceptible to mind, it seems to be on its way to the great King himself. But amid its longing to see him, pure and untempered rays of concentrated light stream forth like a torrent, so that by its gleams the eye of understanding is dazzled.

Please note here "sober intoxication," the image of drunkenness as standing for ecstasy. Please note the acme of the mind; please note the rays of light that shine forth. This is going to come repeatedly in Jewish and Muslim Mysticism. And, finally, it is the "eye of understanding" that is dazzled. It is not a literal light; it is, rather, a light that illumines the mind.

In another passage, he speaks about the fact that even though he is lowly, he is given enough enlightenment and wisdom so that he dares to read the sacred messages of Moses. "And also in my love of knowledge to peer into each of them and unfold and reveal what is not known to the multitude." I seize on this passage because it shows us the continuing importance of the interpretation of Torah in Jewish Mysticism. The mystic is the one who can read the text of Torah and unfold and reveal to others the deeper meanings of the text that are not obvious to the literal minded. Notice again, exoteric and esoteric—the exoteric is the literal meaning of the text; the esoteric are the deeper mystical secrets that the text holds, and only a mystical reading can unfold these.

Philo also speaks in glowing terms of Jewish monks both in Palestine (probably the Essenes) but also some local Jews in Egypt, whom he calls the Therapeutae. And he describes their life:

> They keep the memory of God alive and never forget, it so that even in their dreams the picture is nothing else but the loveliness of divine excellence and power. Indeed many when asleep and dreaming give utterance to the glorious varieties of their holy philosophy.

He says when they pray in the morning, they pray for a bright day, but what they mean by a bright day is the enlightenment of their mind. At night, they pray for a good night, but what they mean by a good night is a night that is filled with thoughts of the divine.

> And all day long, they read Holy Scripture and seek wisdom from their ancestral philosophy by taking it as an allegory,

since they think that the words of the literal text are symbols of something else whose hidden nature is revealed through studying.

What we see in Philo is going to be much more the future of Jewish Mysticism, the seeking in the text of Torah deeper meanings which can reveal realities about God. But the next phase of Jewish Mysticism that we are going to see continues the tradition of *I Enoch* and the monks at Qumran, namely, a preoccupation with the heavenly throne-chariot. And so, in the next phase of Jewish Mysticism, we are going to be taking a glimpse at the riders of the throne-chariot, the practitioners of Merkabah Mysticism.

Lecture Five
Merkabah Mysticism

Scope:

The Judaism that emerged from the Mishnah of Judah the Prince and crystallized in the Babylonian Talmud and the Talmud of the Land of Israel was centered on the observance and study of God's Law. Indeed, the study of the laws of sacrifice was regarded as the equivalent of actually carrying out sacrifices in the Jerusalem temple after its destruction in 70 C.E. Classical Judaism appears at first to be supremely legal and intellectual, yet at the heart of the rabbinic circles was a powerful form of mysticism centered in the spiritual "ascent" to the heavenly throne-chariot (*merkabah*). This form of mysticism had its dangers and was, therefore, restricted to the holiest and most learned among the rabbis.

Outline

I. The classical form of Judaism that emerged from centuries of turbulence was firmly based on the community's observance of God's Law.

    A. The convictions of the Pharisees and the expertise of the scribes fused with a diaspora setting to shape a tradition that endured for 1,800 years.

        1. The Pharisees began as one of the first sects in Judaism, who made the observance of God's Law, the Torah, their central commitment.

        2. The ancient laws written in Scripture (TaNaK) could be extended and contemporized through the use of "midrash" (interpretation) applied to legal material (Halakah) or non-legal material (Haggadah).

        3. This oral Torah (or second Torah) allowed a highly flexible form of life for a people forced to live among those not sharing their convictions.

        4. As it developed, this Jewish tradition placed equal emphasis on carrying out the Commandments and studying them; both equally honored God.

    B. The tradition expressed itself in an incremental body of literature focused on the Law of God.

1. The Mishnah of Judah ha-Nasi (c. 200 C.E.), composed in classical Hebrew, codified an oral tradition based on interpretation of Scripture and provided the basis for all subsequent development.
2. *The Talmud of the Land of Israel* (4th century) and *The Babylonian Talmud* (5th or 6th century) added commentary to the Mishnah in Aramaic (Gemara); the Babylonian version became the normative text for Jews over the next centuries.
3. The conversations among these rabbis continued in collections of material that had not previously been anthologized and in further commentaries on the Talmud itself.

C. Classical Judaism was a way of life shaped by the word of God as adapted to ever-changing circumstances.
1. Obeying God's Commandments was not only a matter of individual but also of community obligation: Torah showed adherents how to walk (Halakah).
2. Community worship (for example, on the Sabbath) also focused on Torah. The Sabbath offered freedom from work to study Torah.
3. The divine presence (Shekinah) is particularly felt among those who study Torah.

II. The Babylonian Talmud shows us the early development of a mysticism centered on the heavenly throne-chariot (*merkabah*) in the heart of the rabbinic tradition.

A. Under the rubric of forbidden relations (Lev. 18:6), the Mishnah passage in the Babylonian Talmud tractate *Hagigah* 11b shifts to esoteric teaching.
1. Speculation on "the work of the creation and the work of the chariot" is restricted to sages.
2. Speculation on "four things … what is above, what is beneath, what before, what after" is strictly forbidden.

B. As the Talmud continues, we find that by no means was the prohibition or careful qualification of these subjects the only opinion. The Gemara discussion is much more open to the presence of this kind of mystical speculation.
1. The Gemara discusses the meaning of the seventh heaven, the creatures around the throne, and the chambers in heaven.

2. It also speculates on the size of the bodies of the heavenly creatures that appeared to Ezekiel.
3. The Gemara notes, however, that its speculation on the throne-chariot can be undertaken only by those who are most learned and most observant of the Torah.
4. In the Talmud, speculation of this sort seems to give rise to miracles.

C. The two characteristics of this mysticism as found in the Talmud, then, are that such speculation is forbidden to the many and is restricted to the most learned and pious.

III. In the production of *Hekaloth* literature (edited in the 5th through 6th centuries), there is evidence for a vigorous practice of mysticism centered in ascent to the divine presence.

A. This literature (*III Enoch, The Lesser Hekaloth, The Greater Hekaloth*) describes the heavenly halls or palaces through which the visionary passes. In the seventh heaven is the throne-chariot on which God sits.
1. The mystical ascent is always preceded by ascetical practices over a period of 12 to 40 days.
2. Angelic gatekeepers seek to prevent the ascent and must be placated by prayers, seals, or passwords, such as proper verses from the Torah.
3. The higher the ascent, the greater the dangers grow. Of course, the ascent is an internal rather than an external one.
4. The dangers include gazing on the waters, passing through fire, and experiencing suspension in bottomless space.

B. Certain recurrent elements appear in the *Hekaloth* literature, distinguishing it from the midrashic tradition.
1. The visions of the throne-chariot and heavenly chambers are imaginative expansions of the clues given by Scripture.
2. The emphasis on God's transcendence is mitigated by *Shiur Koma* (measure of the body), speculation on the body of God (perhaps derived from the Song of Songs).
3. The "garment of light" serves both to reveal and to conceal the presence of God.

4. Heavenly hymns are low on specific content but rhetorically rich and constitute the distinct prayer component in this mysticism.

IV. In a tradition that seems totally exoteric—completely focused on keeping the Law—there appears an esoteric teaching, a *sod*, a secret, practiced by those who had the greatest stake and expertise in the external forms.

    A. The literature and social setting alike require us to think in terms of a school tradition.

    B. The spiritual (internal) ascent of the mind and heart, together with the ascetical preparation, reveal that the point of the Law is a relationship of the individual person with God.

    C. The emphasis in this scholastic circle remains on the mind more than on the heart; the language is speculative more than affective.

    D. There is a strong possibility that the writing of this literature is itself a medium by which the experience is sought.

Recommended Reading:

Scholem, G. *Major Trends in Jewish Mysticism*, pp. 40–79.

Questions to Consider:

1. How does the rabbinic practice of Merkabah Mysticism illustrate the relationship between the esoteric and exoteric in religion?

2. Discuss the theme of "danger" posed by mystical ascent to those uninitiated or uninstructed.

Lecture Five—Transcript
Merkabah Mysticism

In the last lecture, we saw how between the religion of ancient Israel, which is depicted in the Hebrew Bible, and classical Judaism, the study of which I take up today, there was a turbulent period of self-definition lasting more than 500 years, as Jews sought—in the face of powerful cultural forces (Hellenistic culture) and political realities (Roman rule)—to find the way to honor God through the observance of Torah. Even in that period of crisis, we caught glimpses of powerful mystical experience and expression. In this presentation, I take up the emergence of classical Judaism and its characteristic form of mysticism.

The term "classical Judaism" refers to the form of Judaism that lasted from the year 200 really until the present day. It is also called Talmudic Judaism on the basis of the compositions that form its basis, or rabbinic Judaism, named for the teachers within this tradition called "rabbis," (masters). It emerged from these centuries of turbulence firmly committed to the community's observance of God's Law. And three factors combined to form this religion that we now called Judaism. It was the conviction of the Pharisees, the expertise of the scribes, and a diaspora setting. These joined together to shape a tradition that endured for some 1,800 years. After the destruction of the Temple in the year 70 C.E. and especially after the destruction of the city of Jerusalem by the Romans in the year 135, the flexible and creative convictions of the Pharisees enabled Judaism to survive and even thrive as a minority cult.

The Pharisees began as one of those first sects in Judaism who made the observance of God's Law, the Torah, their central commitment. They were less concerned with the kingship, or the land, or the temple. They were committed to all pious Jews observing all of God's Commandments. The problem with that commitment is that God's Laws were written a long time ago for other circumstances. How can one extend ancient laws to contemporary circumstances, to changing circumstances? How can you take words that were spoken through Moses for agricultural realities to new urban realities? Here is where the expertise of the scribes comes into play. The scribes, *ha sopherim,* the "men of the book," were able to interpret the laws through a process called "midrash." The term "midrash" comes from the Hebrew verb *darash,* which means simply "to search out" or "to seek." And the scribes sought in every word, every syllable, every letter of the Hebrew text of Scripture a way to get leverage for contemporizing ancient laws for new circumstances. When they applied this expertise to legal materials—actual laws—the form of midrash was called halakic midrash, from the Hebrew verb Halakah, "to walk." Observe—if it is applied to the stories of the Bible, or to the Psalms, or to wisdom literature, it is called haggadic midrash, from haggadah, meaning "to recite," basically.

This process of interpretation formed what is called in Judaism the oral Torah or even the second Torah. It formed a highly flexible way of life for a people who were forced to live among those not sharing their convictions. Judaism, during all these years, was never a majority population. It was always a minority religion that had to live among people who in no way agreed with their central convictions. An example of the flexibility of this: The Laws of Moses require of landowners to reserve a corner of their fields (called the *pe'ah*) and to leave it unharvested so that a sojourner in the land (an orphan, a widow, people who did not have property and who might otherwise starve to death) could glean that corner of the field and, thus, sustain themselves. Midrash enabled the Pharisees and scribes, the rabbis, to translate that ancient agricultural norm concerning the corner of a field into a complex and sophisticated welfare system for Jewish communities throughout the world, wherever they were—a soup kitchen for those who had daily needs, a community chest that made resources available on a more extended basis for people whose needs were more complicated. As it developed, this Jewish tradition placed equal emphasis on the doing of the Commandments and on the study of the Commandments. Study was highly valorized within this tradition. Both equally honored God. Take, for example, the laws of sacrifice. There are many laws pertaining to the sacrifice of animals in the Temple in Jerusalem, but after the destruction of the Temple, it is obviously no longer possible to carry out actual sacrifices. How can a pious Jew continue to observe those laws that God placed upon the people? The answer is obvious. We study the laws of sacrifice as they are found in the Bible. We seek to understand them. And this is regarded as the equivalent of carrying out the sacrifices. So you see how study becomes, in fact, the equivalent of the observance. And this study of the laws of sacrifice was the form, in rabbinic Judaism, of spiritual sacrifices offered to God.

This tradition expressed itself in an ever-expanding collection of literature. The first major stage is the codification of the Law by Judah ha-Nasi, Judah the Prince, around the year 200. It is written in classical Hebrew, and it is called the Mishnah. The Mishnah gathers together the prior history of interpretation carried out by scribes and organizes it into what is, in effect, a law book. It is organized according to topics. The Mishnah in classical Hebrew becomes the basis for all subsequent developments in rabbinic Judaism. The first developments were two bodies of lore called the Talmud—in the plural, Talmudim. There is *The Talmud of the Land of Israel* (sometimes called the Palestinian Talmud) that comes from the 4th century, and *The Talmud of Babylon* (the Babylonian Talmud) from the 5th or 6th centuries. The Talmud is a collection of commentary (Gemara in Aramaic) on the Mishnah. What we see, then, is a continuing scholarly conversation about God's Law. The Mishnah is the basis; scholars continue to debate that Law; and the results of their debates are then put into a composition called the Talmud. *The Talmud of Babylon* is the one that was normative for Jews for many, many centuries, which attests to the high esteem in which Babylonian Judaism was held by Jews throughout the world. Babylon, of course, is present-day Iraq, and the Jewish community in southern Iraq was the center for rabbinic thought for centuries.

The conversations between these rabbis didn't stop with the publication of the Talmudim. These conversations continued in collections of material that had not previously been anthologized and in further commentaries on the Talmud itself. All of this vast body of lore, which has its origin in the ancient Scripture, the Torah, which feeds into the Mishnah and then expands incrementally into the Talmudim and even further into commentaries on the Talmudim, forms the basis for rabbinic Judaism and is called the "ocean of the Talmud," a phrase that is well chosen, I think.

Classical Judaism was a way of life shaped by the word of God as adapted to ever-changing circumstances. Obeying God's Commandments was not only a matter of individual but also of community obligation. Torah shows us how to walk, Halakah. Community worship, for example, on the Sabbath also focused on Torah—the reading of Torah, the singing of Torah, and yes, the study of Torah. Sabbath represented a freedom from profane work in order to carry out that playful work which was the study of Torah. And in this tradition—and I'm beginning to make a move to mysticism now—there was a strong conviction that the Shekinah (the word means "shadow of presence"; it's the term used for the divine presence among humans) is particularly present among those who are studying Torah. There is a saying that when two or three are gathered together to study Torah, there is the Shekinah among them. And a saying attributed to Rabbi Hillel is: "If even one occupies himself in the study of Torah, there is the Shekinah." And there was a wonderful midrash on the Song of Songs where you can imagine a gazelle leaping from hill to hill across Galilee, and the rabbis interpret this as the Shekinah leaping from synagogue to synagogue across Galilee wherever Jews are gathered to study Torah. So we have a strong connection, which is going to be consistent in this tradition, between reading Torah and God's presence. This will be at the heart of all Jewish Mysticism as we continue.

The scholarly question is: Was this only about Law, or was there a mysticism, an esoteric sort of teaching that went on even at the heart of the rabbinic tradition? And here is where the great work of Gershom Scholem, to which I have referred before and will refer again, is so important, because he draws us all the way back to the Talmud itself to show us the beginnings of a development of a mysticism that is based on the heavenly throne-chariot, which we have met before in the visions of Ezekiel, and that takes place at the very heart of the rabbinic tradition.

In the Babylonian Talmud tractate *Hagigah*, beginning in 11b, we have the statement of the Mishnah that begins with the subject of forbidden relations. The main topic is the kinds of sexual relations that are forbidden by the book of Leviticus in chapter 18, but in a characteristic rabbinic associative thinking, the subject of forbidden sexual relations moves rather quickly to other kinds of boundary breaking, other kinds of forbidden things, and the topic quickly moves to forbidden topics of conversation. And we find there in the Mishnah that there is a prohibition of expounding

> the "work of the creation and the work of the Chariot in the presence of one, unless he is a sage and understanding of his own knowledge." ... [And it continues.] "Whoever speculates on four things what is above, what is beneath, what before, what after and takes no thought for the honor of his Maker, it were a mercy if he had not come into the world."

What we have here, then, in the Mishnah, is the absolute prohibition of one kind of speculation, which seems to be theosophical or Gnostic. What happened before the world? What happens after the world? What's above the world? What's beneath it? That's forbidden. And then there's a careful qualifying of two other things: what is creation about and the throne-chariot. This is a mystical speculation that we found already in works like *I Enoch*.

As the Talmud continues, then, we find that by no means was the prohibition of these subjects or the careful qualification of these subjects the only opinion. We see that there is a lot of speculation going on. The negative tone of the Mishnah is not matched by the positive tone of the Gemara. In other words, the continuing Aramaic discussion is much more open to the presence of this kind of mystical speculation. There's a discussion of the meaning of the seventh heaven. There is a discussion of the creatures around the throne. There's a discussion of the chambers in heaven. Chambers— do we remember the *hekal*, the heavenly palace where God's throne is? And then there's speculation on the size of the bodies of the heavenly creatures that appeared to Ezekiel. There is a lot of speculation going on in these circles. The Gemara then continues to say that its speculation on the throne-chariot can only be undertaken by those who are most learned and most observant of the Torah. It was only for the initiate, but for them it was, the Talmud says, "honey under the tongue." For the uninitiated, it was hazardous and even fatal. And so we see that this mystical speculation on the throne-chariot and on the heavens was taking place at the very heart of the rabbinic tradition, and the mystics were the ones who were the most learned and the most observant of the exoteric tradition. In this case, the esoteric and the exoteric are very closely linked.

Another thing we observe as we continue in the Talmud is that speculation of this sort seems to give rise to miracles. We have the story of Johanan ben Zakkai and Eleazar ben Allach, who were discussing the throne-chariot when the heavens opened up and fire spilled out on the Earth. In another incident, two rabbis are discussing this topic, and the sunny weather changes to cloudy weather, and the angels listen in on the exposition. The angels are overhearing the rabbis discuss them, in effect. And when Johanan ben Zakkai heard this last story, he tells his listeners of a dream that he himself had had in which a heavenly voice had said to him, "Ascend hither. Ascend hither." Johanan ben Zakkai is at the very beginning of the rabbinic tradition. He is one of the great heroes in classical Judaism, and here we have him claiming that he received a revelation from God to ascend in this fashion.

What we have, then, is this speculation going on, and the Talmud then moves to one of the most famous stories about this kind of ascent. It is called the story of the four who entered the garden, and it begins, "Our rabbis taught." This phrase in the Talmud usually indicates that this tradition goes all the way back to the time of the Tannaim the very first Talmudic students, probably in the 1st or 2nd century C.E. "Our rabbis taught. Four entered an orchard, and these are they: Ben 'Azzai, Ben Zoma, Aher, and Rabbi Akiva." Rabbi Akiva is the supreme hero of this tradition. Rabbi Akiva was the most learned of rabbis. He was a martyr. He died in the Bar Kochba Revolt, having declared Bar Kochba the Messiah, and was executed by the Romans. As he was killed, he cried out the Shema Yisrael: "Hear, O Israel, the Lord your God is one," and on that final *echad*, or "one," he expired. There is no hero in the tradition more orthodox, more certified than Rabbi Akiva, and he's one of the four who enter into the garden.

Rabbi Akiva said to them, when you reach the stones of pure marble, do not say "Water, water." Do you remember that shiny floor that we talked about in previous lectures? When you reach the shiny floor, do not cry out, "Water, water."

> For it is said: "He that speaketh of falsehood should not be established before mine eyes." Ben 'Azzai gazed and died. Of him Scripture says: "Precious in the sight of the Lord is the death of his saints." Ben Zoma gazed and was stricken. Of him, Scripture says: "Hast thou found honey? Eat as much as is sufficient for thee, lest thou be filled therewith and vomited." [So one died; one got sick.] Aher cut down the shoots.

Aher is a famous heretic in the Jewish tradition, and he did damage when he entered into the mystical realm. Rabbi Akiva, the fourth, departed in peace. The story is a wonderful illustration of the hazards, the dangers, of engaging in this kind of mystical enterprise without proper preparation, without proper learning. The two characteristics of this mysticism as found in the Talmud, then, are that such speculation is forbidden to the many and is restricted to the most learned and pious. It truly is esoteric, but it is practiced thoroughly by those who are exoterically qualified.

During this period of classical Judaism, we have the production of a great amount of what is called *Hekaloth* literature, which was edited in the 5th through the 6th centuries. Again, this term is based upon that word *hekal*, or palace. There is evidence for a vigorous practice of mysticism in rabbinic schools centered in the ascent to the divine presence. These *Hekaloth* books—*III Enoch, The Lesser Hekaloth, The Greater Hekaloth*—describe the heavenly halls or palaces through which the visionary passes. In the seventh of these heavens is the throne-chariot, where God is present. The *Third Book of Enoch*, one of the *Hekaloth* writings, begins in this fashion. First, it quotes Genesis: "Enoch walked with God, then he vanished, because God took him," that I referred to earlier.

Rabbi Ishmael is another great hero of the tradition who died before 132 C.E. And then Rabbi Ishmael said, "When I ascended to the height to behold the vision of the chariot, I entered six palaces, one inside the other, and when I reached the door of the seventh palace, I paused in prayer before the Holy One, blessed be he." And so he prays to God that the opposing angels not stop him from accomplishing his ascent, because in this tradition, there are angels who seek to protect the divine presence and want to prevent humans from entering into that presence. So Ishmael prays to God, and God sends the angel Metatron, who is the angel who stands beside the throne, who says to Ishmael:

> "Come in peace into the presence of the high and exalted King, to behold the likeness of the chariot." Then I entered the seventh palace, and he led me to the camp of the Shekinah [to the divine presence] and presented me before the throne of glory, so that I might behold the chariot. [So there he is in the presence of the divine.] But after an hour, the Holy One, blessed be he, opened to me the gates of Shekinah, gates of peace, gates of wisdom, gates of strength, gates of might, gates of speech, gates of song, gates of sanctity and praise, gates of chant. [You hear the mystical repetition of these kinds of words.] He enlightened my eyes and my heart to utter psalm, praise, jubilation, thanksgiving, song, glory, majesty, laud, and strength. And when I opened my mouth and sang praises before the throne of glory, the

holy creatures below the throne of glory and above the throne responded after me, saying: Holy, holy, holy and, Blessed be the glory of the Lord in his dwelling place.

This mystical ascent undertaken by the rabbi is always preceded by ascetical practices, ranging from 12 to 40 days—that is, fasting, strict observance of Torah, and immediately before the ascent, abstinence from sexual relations. Angelic gatekeepers, as I've suggested, seek to prevent the ascent and must be placated by prayers, or seals, or passwords, such as knowing the proper verses of Torah. And the higher you go in the ascent, the more dangerous it is. We are speaking, of course, about an internal rather than external ascent, you will remember. The idea is that you're thinking of ascending, but in some sense, you're also descending into interiority, and the further you go into that, the more dangerous it is. The dangers include gazing on the waters, passing through fires, experiencing suspension in bottomless space.

Certain recurrent elements appear in this *Hekaloth* literature that make it distinct within the midrashic tradition. The visions of the throne-chariot and the heavenly chambers are an imaginative expansion of the clues that are given by Scripture. We find, in what might be the very first example of Merkabah Mysticism, a work called "The Vision of Ezekiel." It's talking about the scriptural passage. It should have said heaven was opened. Why does it say the heavens were opened? This is a classic rabbinic move, paying attention to every single word in Scripture. Why doesn't it simply say heaven was opened; why does it say "the heavens" were opened? Well, it must mean that there's more than one heaven. This teaches that seven heavens were open to Ezekiel—*Shamayyim, Shemei ha-Shamayyim, Zevul, Araphel, Shehakim, Aravot*, and the Throne of Glory. Why are there these seven heavens? To protect Ezekiel and his readers from the assumption that access to God is immediate or quick, that you can simply see God. The effect of this Merkabah Mysticism is twofold. On the one side, it is an arduous effort to make that contact. On the other side, it is an effort to protect the transcendence of God. God is not going to be reached simply by desiring it. We see in this same composition that the author says that there is a 500-year journey between heaven number 1 and heaven number 2, and a 500-year journey between numbers 2 and 3, and so forth. So it's going to take about 3,500 years for you to reach the actual presence of God. This is an effort to say that God really is other. Mysticism is an arduous, difficult process; it is not something you can do with the snap of your fingers.

This emphasis on God's transcendence, which I do think characterizes Merkabah Mysticism, is somewhat mitigated by another feature, which is called *Shiur Koma*—literally, the "measure of the body." It's very odd, and I bring it up because it's going to recur throughout the tradition. It's speculation on God's body and the measurement of God's body. There are all of these extravagant—just like those 500-year journeys—numbers describing, if you will, God's limbs in cosmic terms. It is an effort to overcome that notion of transcendence with a sense of immanence, that God is utterly different than us, but there is some way in which God has a body as we have a body. This may come from speculation on the Song of Songs, where we saw there was a preoccupation with the body of the beloved. In this literature, as well, there is the garment of light that serves both to conceal and to reveal the presence of God. And as I read from *III Enoch*, there is the presence of heavenly hymns that give a numinous glow to the whole process, even though they are rather low on specific content: "Holy, holy, holy is the Lord of Hosts."

Within this rabbinic tradition, in a tradition that seemed totally exoteric, totally about keeping the Law, there appears an esoteric teaching, a *sod*, a secret, practiced by those who had the greatest stake and expertise in the external forms. The literature and social setting alike require us to think in terms of a school tradition. Remember, before the time of printing, you could only read Torah in manuscript, which meant that scholars had to gather in the same room and read together. So you have the social context for this kind of exoteric and esoteric reading. The spiritual or internal ascent of the mind and heart, together with ascetical preparation, is a way of asserting that the point of the Law is a relationship of the individual person with God. The emphasis in this scholastic circle remains more on the mind than it does on the heart. The language is more speculative than it is affective. There is the strong possibility that the writing of this literature, as I have suggested before, is itself a medium by which the experience is sought. In the next presentation, we will look at a further development in Jewish Mysticism in which the heart, much more than the mind, will be emphasized.

Lecture Six
The Hasidim of Medieval Germany

Please be advised that parts of this lecture contain some explicit discussion of sexual matters and may be unsuitable for children.

Scope:

Life for Jews in the Christendom of medieval Europe was not easy. For Jews in Germany from 1150–1250, dedication to the keeping of Torah was particularly perilous, because Christian Crusade fever could extend itself easily to Jewish neighbors. In these constrained circumstances and under the threat of persecution, a form of mysticism developed that appealed even to Jews who were not great scholars. The *Sefer Hasidim* (*Book of the Devout*) affirmed the centrality of Torah and had connections with the earlier Merkabah tradition but was characterized by commitment to a deep personal piety that eschewed messianic speculation and emphasized altruistic love as the essence of obedience to God.

Outline

I. This lecture explores a form of Jewish Mysticism that is quieter, more grounded in common life, less speculative, and more rooted in the heart than the Merkabah tradition—the mysticism of the Hasidim in medieval Germany.

   A. In the period of the ascendance of Christendom in Europe, Christianity pervaded all social and political structures, and various laws ensured that Jews remained separate within society and, thus, at risk.
       1. Jews were not legally able to own land, and in a feudal society based in landowning, this meant that their livelihood was restricted to trade and finance.
       2. Economically, therefore, Jews were both necessary (Christians were forbidden to practice usury) and resented.

   B. Although there were moments of cooperation (as between the biblical scholars Rashi and Hugh of St. Victor in the 11th century), the dominant atmosphere was hostile and oppressive.

1. Popular anti-Semitism, fed by Christian preaching, broke out in times of stress, as in the First Crusade (1096–1099).
2. States could expel Jews at will, as France did in 1182 and Spain in 1492. Further, the church issued controlling laws, as did the Fourth Lateran Council in 1215, and sponsored the burning of the Talmud on many occasions.

C. Despite such external pressures, life in the Jewish community remained faithful to its religious roots.
1. With the schools (yeshivah) held in local synagogues, generations of scholars continued the reading of Torah in Hebrew and Aramaic and passed on mystical traditions.
2. In his last will and testament, Eleazar of Mainz (d. 1357), an ordinary Jewish businessman, testifies to the widespread practice of piety.

II. In medieval Germany a distinctive form of mysticism developed from 1150–1250 called the *Hasidei Ashkenazi* (the "Devout" or "Pious of Germany").

A. This strain of mysticism was shaped by three generations of teachers from the same family, the Kalonymides.
1. Samuel the Hasid was the son of Kalonymus of Speyer and lived in the middle of the 12th century; little of his writing remains.
2. His son was Jehudah the Hasid of Worms, who died in Regensburg in 1217; his many writings are now known only through his disciples, although he was regarded virtually as a prophet.
3. Eleazar ben Jehudah of Worms (1160–1238) has left the greatest body of literature and is the main source of our knowledge about this form of Jewish Mysticism.

B. Among Eleazar ben Jehudah's works, the most influential is *Sefer Hasidim* (the *Book of the Devout*, or the *Book of the Pious*).
1. Its teaching shows lines of continuity with earlier Jewish traditions, including Merkabah and the writings of the 10th-century scholar Saadia Gaon, who stressed the analogy between divine and human love.

2. It is also possible to find the influence of Christian Mysticism in Jehudah's work, for example, in the emphasis on penitence.

III. This German Mysticism was both more popular than Merkabah and less speculative, focusing on the shaping of individuals as pious.

A. Mysticism became a practice for ordinary Jews, not only for those in small scholarly groups.

1. The hasid need not be a person of towering intellect or a scholar but simply a humble searcher after holiness.
2. The hasid can, nevertheless, become a guide to others on the path of piety and can accomplish astounding deeds, as in the creation of the golem.
3. The pious person can even receive by direct inspiration the solution to legal problems that confound scholars.

B. Mysticism is focused not on the outer world of history but on the inner life of the devout individual.

1. Messianic speculation is discouraged if not forbidden; it is a distraction from personal transformation.
2. Thinking about the end time concerns not the Messiah but the personal destiny of the individual.
3. There is a great focus on prayer, which involves a concern for the motives of the Commandments and the precise words (including their numerical values) used in prayer.

C. Three aspects of such personal piety in the *Book of the Devout* resemble the stages of mystical progression in other traditions.

1. The hasid practices physical asceticism that takes the form of a renunciation of the pleasures offered by the world. This can involve a pervasive commitment to penitence.
2. The hasid practices serenity of mind in all circumstances, even those of persecution.
3. The hasid practices an altruism—justice toward other humans—that goes beyond the demands of the Law.

IV. The theosophy (speculation about the divine realm) among the Hasidim is not systematically coherent but emphasizes the human relationship to an immanent God.

A. God remains the transcendent one of the earlier tradition, but now, we see a development of God's attributes as aspects of divine immanence.

    1. The Pious Ones of Germany interpret the traditional attributes of God—that he is wise, is holy, has glory, and has a presence—as ways of bringing God closer to us.

    2. Heavenly archetypes exist for all created things, including humans, who can work to realize their heavenly ideal.

B. Corresponding to the closeness of the divine is an emphasis on love even more than knowledge.

    1. Human erotic love may be an expression of the love between humans and God; there is no sexual asceticism in this form of piety.

    2. This form of mysticism affirms human erotic love, and it is an analogy to the love between God and humans but only an analogy.

Recommended Reading:

Scholem, G. *Major Trends in Jewish Mysticism*, pp. 80–118.

Questions to Consider:

1. How does German Hasidism broaden our understanding of what mysticism can include?

2. Discuss how a "spirit of penitence" can be compatible with a robust and joyful celebration of human sexuality.

Lecture Six—Transcript
The Hasidim of Medieval Germany

Our first glimpse of mysticism in the rabbinic tradition had all the elements of esotericism we might desire—a small group of scholars gathered around biblical texts, disciplining themselves for a dangerous mystical ascent or descent through prayer and fasting, and returning with elaborate portrayals of the heavenly courts and the divine throne-chariot. Our next glimpse reveals another strain of Jewish Mysticism, one that is quieter, more grounded in common life, less speculative, and more rooted in the heart. This is the mysticism of the Hasidim in medieval Germany.

We should approach this new development in Jewish Mysticism by first appreciating its historical context. The story of Judaism in the Christian Middle Ages is one of intense creativity within severely constrained circumstances. We are in the period in Europe called Christendom, when Christianity pervaded all social and political structures. Various laws ensured that Jews remained separate within society and, as separate, at risk. Jews, for example, were not legally able to own land. In a feudal society based in landowning, when land was the measure of one's social position, this meant that Jews were restricted for their survival to trade and to finance. Therefore, economically, Jews were both necessary, since Christians were not allowed to practice usury—that is, to loan money at interest—and, therefore, they needed to turn to Jewish money lenders in order to acquire capital. So they were necessary, but they were also deeply resented.

Although there were moments of cooperation between Jews and Christians in this medieval period, as between the biblical scholars Rashi and Hugh of St. Victor in the 11th century, the dominant atmosphere was hostile and oppressive. Popular anti-Semitism, fed by Christian preaching that exploited the so-called blood curse brought upon the Jews in the Gospel of Matthew and slanders concerning the murdering of children and the poisoning of wells— these sorts of things broke out in times of stress, leading to very dangerous times for Jews.

As an example, in the First Crusade against the infidels, the Muslims, in the year 1096, ignorant Christians on their way to do battle in the Holy Land began to slaughter Jews in small European towns as they made their way across the countryside, failing to distinguish between the infidels who were Muslims and the infidels who were Jews, infidels in their eyes. States could expel Jews at will, as France did in 1182 and Spain did in 1492. The church issued controlling laws, as the Fourth Lateran Council did in the year 1215, and sponsored the burning of the Talmud on many occasions. Imagine—burning the Talmud is burning the very basis of a community's life. Christian rulers would hold public debates between appointed rabbis and Christian missionaries; the ostensible reason for the debates was for the purposes of conversion, but the real reason was to make sure that Jews were always conspicuous by their difference and, therefore, always liable and to be dealt with.

Despite such external pressures, life within the Jewish community remained impressively faithful to its religious roots. With the schools, the yeshivah, that were held in local synagogues, generations of scholars continued the reading of Torah in Hebrew and the Talmud in Aramaic. In the same social context of study, as I have suggested, were passed on mystical traditions. We can see the vibrancy of this medieval Jewish life in a wonderful last will and testament written by an ordinary Jewish businessman, Eleazar of Mainz, who died in the year 1357, which testifies to the widespread practice of piety among Jews. This address is to his children:

> These are things which my sons and daughters shall do at my request. They shall go to the house of prayer morning and evening and shall pay special regard to the prayer and to the *Shema* [the confession of faith]. As soon as the service is over, they shall occupy themselves a little with Torah, the Psalms or with works of charity. Their business, must be conducted honestly, in their dealings both with Jew and with gentile. They must be gentle in the manners and prompt to accede to every honorable request. They must not talk more than is necessary, by this will they be saved from slander, falsehood, and frivolity. They shall never turn away a poor man empty handed, but must give him what they can, be it much or little.

And then he turns to the specific obligations of his male and female children.

> My daughters must obey scrupulously the rules applying to women. … In their relationship with women, my sons must

behave continently, avoiding mixed bathing and mixed dancing, and all frivolous conversations.

And he goes on giving his children a moral testament, what he expects of them as people who adhere to God's Commandments. And he says, "Every one of these good qualities becomes habitual with him who studies the Torah." So you see that the studying of the Torah, the purpose of it, is to engender a good character:

> For that study indeed leads to the formation of a noble character. Therefore, happy is he who toils in the Law! For this gracious toil, fixed daily times of long or short duration, for it is the best of all works that a man can do.

I want to read you one more sentence or so out of this wonderful text:

> Be of the first ten in the synagogue [get to church early], rising betimes for the purpose. Pray steadily with the congregation, giving due value to every letter and word, seeing that there are in the *Shema* [the statement of faith] 248 words corresponding to the 248 limbs in the human body.

This is a throwaway line. And he then proceeds to give instructions about his funeral and so forth, but I want you to pay attention to the fact of the connection between the limbs of the human body and the numbers that are found in Torah; this will become important in mystical literature.

In medieval Germany, a distinctive form of mysticism developed between 1150 and 1250 called the *Hasidei Ashkenazi*, the "Devout" or the "Pious Ones of Germany." Its creative shaping is due, above all, to three generations of teachers within the same family, the Kalonymides. Samuel the Hasid, Samuel the Pious, was the son of Kalonymus of Speyer and lived in the middle of the 12th century. Little of his writing remains. His son was Jehudah the Hasid of Worms, who died in Regensburg in 1217. His many writings are now known only as they have been anthologized by his disciples, although he was regarded virtually as a prophet by those disciples. And, finally, the third generation, Eleazar ben Jehudah of Worms, whose dates are 1160–1238—he has left us the largest body of literature and is the main source of our knowledge about this form of Jewish Mysticism. Among Eleazar ben Jehudah's works, the most influential is the one called *Sefer Hasidim*, the *Book of the Devout*, or the *Book of the Pious*. Please notice the very choice of words. It's not the *Book of the Speculators* or the *Book of the Higher Mystics*; it's the *Book of the Devout*. And from the beginning of this course, I have emphasized that the topic of mysticism includes not only the great theosophical speculations and the ascents into heaven but also the life of devotion that is found among people.

The teaching of Eleazar ben Jehudah shows lines of continuity with earlier Jewish traditions. We do have elements of Merkabah Mysticism found in his work. We also, fascinatingly, find traces of a 10th-century author named Saadia Gaon, Saadia the Great, whose dates are 892–942. What's fascinating about this is that Jehudah drew over Saadia Gaon's analogy between divine love and human love, this sort of erotic dimension that I've spoken of before. But the way to that is peculiar, because Saadia Gaon was a philosophical rationalist; he was far from being a mystic. His main work is *The Book of Philosophic Doctrines and Religious Beliefs*, and it was written in Arabic. So we see the way in which, already in the 9th and 10th centuries, Jewish scholars were turning to Muslim scholars to answer them. But then Saadia Gaon's work was translated into Hebrew—or should I say mistranslated into Hebrew?—and in the Hebrew version, it appeared not as a rationalistic philosophy but as a mystical text. And so it was read this way by Eleazar ben Jehudah.

Another possible connection or influence on Eleazar ben Jehudah was contact with Christian mystics. And the reason for thinking this is because we have an element entering into his mysticism that had not been there before, which is an emphasis on penitence or repentance. Not simply a turning away from sin (that has always been a feature of Judaism) but a lingering remorse, a sense of having to expiate for one's sins, and so forth. Everything that goes in the term "penitence" emerges here as part of this form of mysticism.

How does this mysticism look? It is both more popular than the Merkabah and less speculative. It focuses on the shaping of individuals as pious, as devout. Mysticism becomes a practice for ordinary Jews and not only for those who work in scholarly groups. The hasid is not the extraordinary adept but, rather, the ordinary devout person, precisely the kind of people that were described in the last will and testament that I read, ordinary Jews of Germany. The hasid need not be a person of towering intellect or a scholar but can be simply a humble searcher after holiness. The hasid can, nevertheless, become a guide to others on the path of piety and can accomplish astounding deeds.

Here we find in this literature, remarkably, an element of magic, or theurgy, particularly involving the creation of the golem. The term "golem" refers to a human-like creature who consists entirely of matter, not of mind, who will do one's bidding, sort of a sorcerer's apprentice figure. And the golem has taken on a long life in subsequent Western literature, but it begins right here. Apparently, it begins as something that one imagines in states of prayer and ecstasy and then is believed to actually have a form outside those states of ecstasy. But it is clear throughout the history of Jewish Mysticism that the line between mystery and magic is a very thin one. And where they come together is in the working of miracles, in performance of deeds, what we call later Practical Mysticism. The term "Practical Mysticism" often comes to mean the ability to do extraordinary things.

Another aspect of the extraordinary is the conviction that the pious person can even receive by divine inspiration the solution to legal problems that confound scholars. To provide some background to this text that I will read next, I have to alert you to a tradition in the Jewish literature that is called responsa. When Jews of a community were puzzled by a particular observance of the Law—"What should we do?"—they would turn to a great scholar, even at a great distance, and ask that scholar's opinion. The form of that opinion was a responsum, a "response," so this form of literature is called responsa literature. The most outstanding example we have is the responsum of the great Rav Amram Gaon in Babylon, who wrote to the Jews in Spain, who had asked him about how they should worship. And his responsum to the Jews in Spain is our first example of a full Jewish liturgical text. This is a complex literary backdrop, but we see here the mystic who is asking God for answers to legal problems:

> I asked another question: Is it permitted to make theurgic [magical] use of the holy name of 42 letters, to conjure the holy angels appointed over Torah to make a man wise in all that he studies and never forget his learning? [Can I exercise magic in order to become a great scholar?] And is it permitted to conjure by means of the name the angels

appointed over wealth and victory over enemies in order to find grace in the eyes of princes? [Can I use magic in order to accomplish social prestige?] Or is it forbidden to use theurgic use of the name for any of these purposes?

Remember, magic is often performed in the name of a god or in the name of a powerful figure. So he's asking, "Can I use God's name for this purpose?"

The response: "Holy, holy, holy is the name of the Lord of hosts. He alone will satisfy all your needs." In other words, you don't study Torah in order to accomplish prestige as a scholar or to accomplish victory over one's enemies. You study it in order to approach the living God and give honor to God.

Mysticism, furthermore, in this tradition, is not focused on the outer world of history but on the inner life of the devout person. Speculation about the Messiah is discouraged if not forbidden. It is regarded as a distraction from personal transformation. The last gasp of Jewish Messianism was Rabbi Akiva's proclamation of Bar Kochba as the true Messiah in the year 135. And then Bar Kochba was killed. The city was destroyed. Jews had no hope of returning at that time to the city or the Temple, and messianic hope will not arise again for several centuries. We'll see it when it emerges. But we see, for example, Jehudah saying this: "If you see one making prophecies about the Messiah, you should know that he deals in witchcraft and has intercourse with demons. He is one of those who seek to conjure with the names of God." The very thing that we saw in our previous text was forbidden.

Now, since they conjure the angels or spirits, these tell them about the Messiah, so as to tempt him to reveal his speculations. And in the end he is shamed, because he has called up the angels and demons and instead, a misfortune occurs at that place. … No one knows anything about the coming of Messiah.

So in *The Book of the Devout*, he absolutely forbids this kind of messianic speculation. Instead, thinking about the end time, eschatology involves not when the Messiah will come—it involves what will happen to me after my death. So the sense of an ending is very much concerned with individual eschatology. Will the pious one go to heaven? Will the one who practices magic and has intercourse with demons go to hell? That's the preoccupation.

This mysticism has a great focus on prayer and a concern for what is called the motives of the Commandments. It's a kind of a psychology—why did God command the things that he commanded?—and trying to get inside the mind of God as revealed in the Commandments. It's very down to earth rather than flying off into heavens. There is also a preoccupation with the precise wording of the Commandments and the precise wording of the prayers, including their numerical value. Here we have a topic which is going to recur over again, and that is the topic of gematria. Gematria is practiced in many languages, but above all, those in which the letters of the alphabet also serve as numbers. The first letter of the Hebrew alphabet is aleph; it is also 1. The second letter is bet; it is also 2, and so forth, so that (the point of this is obvious to you) every word also forms a number. All numbers also form words. There is not only an attention to every syllable, and every consonant, and every vowel marking for its significance (what did God mean?), but the numbers begin to invite us into a mystical significance, into a deeper meaning, and we will see the continuing fascination of the interplay between numbers and words as we move forward in this Jewish Mysticism— all of which, I remind you, is centered in the reading of Torah and the study of Torah. We saw already in an earlier presentation how Philo of Alexandria talked about discovering the deeper, inner meanings of the words through the use of Greek philosophy and allegory. Here, we have another way of doing it, not by invoking Greek philosophy but through the very numbers and letters of the Hebrew text itself.

Three aspects of this personal piety that is found in the *Book of the Devout* resemble stages of mystical progress that we will see in other traditions. First, the hasid practices physical asceticism, which involves renunciation of the pleasures offered by the world. This does not, by the way, mean the renunciation of sexual pleasure (this remains very positive) but of wealth, for example, or gorging, and so forth. And as I suggested, this involves, as well, a pervasive commitment to penitence, to sorrow for sin. The first step is a turning away from something, a turning away from over-involvement in the world. The second step is that the hasid practices serenity of mind in all circumstances, even those of oppression or persecution. In other words, the more detached I am from my possessions, from my pleasures, from the things that cling to me, the more I can be serene when those things are threatened. So a serenity of mind, a calmness, peace of mind is a desired goal. And thirdly, the hasid practices an altruism, a justice toward others that does not consist simply in doing the letter of the Law but goes beyond what the Law requires, including the internal disposition of mercy and justice toward the neighbor. These three steps—turning away, gaining a mental condition, and then returning to the neighbor—we will find again and again in this course on mysticism, and we find it here among the Hasidim.

This form of mysticism does not involve a great deal of theosophy (I borrow this term from Gershom Scholem), that is, speculation about the divine realm or speculation about cosmology. Rather, it emphasizes these practical dimensions of piety. But there are some features of theosophy—for example, an emphasis not on the transcendence of God, how God is distant as in Merkabah, but an emphasis on the immanence of God, how God is close to us. God does remain the transcendent one, to be sure. God is holy. But now there's a development of the notion of God's attributes as aspects of God's immanence. There is a line that Jehudah quotes from Saadia Gaon that says:

> Everything is in Thee and Thou art in everything; Thou fillest every thing and dost encompass it; when everything was created, Thou wast in everything; before everything was created, Thou wast everything.

Here, we have our first intimation of how Monotheism can become Pantheism, how the notion of the oneness of God can actually mean that God is in everything, somehow. And it is this delicate dance between the otherness of God and God's immanence, the oneness of God and God's presence in all things, that will continue to preoccupy every form of mysticism that we consider in these three traditions.

Here, we find that the Pious Ones of Germany take the traditional attributes of God—that God is wise, that God is holy, that God has glory, that God has a presence—and they take those attributes as representing the way in which God is closer to us; in other words, the attributes stand between the otherness of God as holy and us. The attributes bring God closer to us and accessible to the devout person. Another aspect of this is that they begin to think that there must be heavenly archetypes for all created things, including humans, who can then work to accomplish their heavenly ideal. There is an ideal human in heaven that is part of the attributes of God. Otherwise, how could God have created humans if there wasn't some concept of humans with God? And so this represents a sort of an archetype toward which humans can work.

Corresponding to the closeness of the divine is an emphasis, in this mysticism, on love, even more than knowledge. There's a strong sense in which the affections of the human person are a way of approaching God just as truly as the mind. We have both the mind and the heart. Merkabah Mysticism really emphasized the mind. The Hasidim tradition really emphasizes the heart, so human erotic love can express the love between humans and God. There is no sexual asceticism in this form of piety. The Hasidim continue the robust, healthy attitude toward sexuality that we find continuously in the Jewish tradition, very much unlike Christian asceticism, which always has difficulties with sexuality. It affirms human erotic love. It is an analogy to the love between God and humans but only an analogy. I want to close with a wonderful reading that begins, "The root of love is to love the Lord. The soul is full of love bound with the bonds of love in great joy. This joy chases away from his heart all bodily pleasure and worldly delight." This is fascinating, because here we see love drawing us away from pleasure and earthly delight, rather than simply renunciation. It is this greater love that draws us.

> The powerful joy of love seizes his heart so that at all times he thinks, "How can I do the will of God?" The pleasures of his children and the company of his wife are as nothing in comparison with the love of God. Imagine a young man who has not been with a woman for a very long time. He longs for her, his heart burns for her. Imagine his great love and desire when he cohabits with her and how, when his sperm shoots like an arrow, he has so much pleasure. All this is nothing compared with his desire to do the will of God, to bring merit to others, to sanctify himself, to sacrifice his life in love. … The love of Heaven, in his heart, is like the flame attached to the coal. He does not gaze at women. He does not engage in frivolous talk, but he concerns himself only to toil, to do the will of God, and he sings songs in order to become filled with joy in the love of God.

What we find here is not a rejection of human love but a celebration of human love which is so great that it can stand as an image of the even greater love that the mystic has for the one God.

Lecture Seven
The Beginnings of Kabbalah

Scope:

In this lecture, we begin to trace the development of Kabbalism, the form of mysticism that is most identified with Judaism and has had a remarkable longevity, extending down to the present. Although the 13th-century composition called the *Zohar* (*Book of Splendor*) is correctly regarded as the normative text of this tradition, it was preceded by at least a century of spectacular developments in mysticism. This lecture traces some of these efforts and seeks the possible connections among them. The lecture concludes with consideration of the work of Rabbi Abraham Abulafia, who represents a form of mysticism that has been called Prophetic Kabbalism.

Outline

I. The complexity and creativity in medieval Judaism stemmed partly from external challenges and partly from internal factors.

   A. As noted in the last lecture, the mysticism of the *Hasidei Ashkenazi* can be seen as both a response to the threat of Christian oppression and as an integration of some Christian themes.

   B. Moses Maimonides (Moses ben Maimon or Rambam, 1135–1204) sought to preserve the truth, integrity, and vibrancy of Judaism in response to the intellectual challenges of Muslim philosophy.

   1. Like the Christian thinker Thomas Aquinas, Maimonides was controversial because of his rational engagement with Arabic thought. Some attacked him, but others, including the scholar Nachmonides (also called Moses ben Nachman Gerondi, c. 1194–1270), defended him.

   2. The *Guide of the Perplexed* by Maimonides was an attempt to work out a defense for Jewish belief and Jewish practice in light of Arabic intellectual currents.

   C. The earliest stages of Kabbalism reveal an intense desire to respect the past (Kabbalah means "tradition"), together with an intense creativity generated by the socio-religious context

©2008 The Teaching Company.

and the concentration of imagination in small groups of Talmudic scholars in Provence and Spain.

1. Although the 13th-century *Zohar* is correctly regarded as the normative text of this tradition, it was preceded by at least a century of spectacular developments in mysticism.

2. It is possible that some cross-influence took place between Christian dualistic movements, such as those found among the Albigensians and the Cathars, and the development of Jewish Kabbalism, but it's not necessary to posit such influence. The elements of Kabbalism were already present in such movements as Merkabah Mysticism.

II. The assumptions and antecedents to 12th-century developments in Kabbalism help us grasp its many subsequent permutations.

   A. The fundamental assumptions concern the way in which God is present in the world and the human means of engaging that presence.

1. For Talmudic scholars, Torah is not only a text that speaks of God, but it is God speaking. It is not simply a text that speaks of the world; the inspired word of God *is* the world.

2. Scripture contains something of God in every individual word and letter: Everything reveals God at some level.

3. Words and letters have significance numerically, as well as semantically, through the practice of gematria.

4. A mystical connection exists between the world of Scripture and the human person.

   B. The earlier mystical tradition in Judaism anticipated later developments.

1. In Merkabah, we saw the practice of *Shiur Koma*, speculation on God in all of his transcendence in terms of the human body.

2. The *Book of Creation* (*Sefer Yesirah*), a short work written before the 10th century, speaks of the emanations of God as *sefirot*.

III. The first manifestations of Kabbalah in Provence and Spain reveal the contributions of many scholars in a cooperative effort.

A. The *Sefer ha-Bahir* (*The Book of Brilliance*) is an anonymous work that has pivotal significance.

   1. It uses the ancient style of midrash on Scripture to communicate new ideas.

   2. The book introduces the notion of a female component in the divinity through the symbol of the Shekinah.

   3. It speculates on the workings of evil, connecting it especially to material reality.

   4. It organizes the 10 *sefirot* and studies them in great detail.

B. Other scholars also made important contributions to this developing form of mysticism.

   1. Rabbi Isaac the Blind (c. 1160–1235) contributed further speculation on the *sefirot*, creating a panoramic understanding of God and world and introducing the possibility of union (*devequt*) through Kabbalistic study.

   2. The Gerona circle in Catalonia included Moses ben Nachman and Rabbi Azriel, who expounded the relationship between the *sefirot* (emanations from the divine into the world) and *Eyn Sof* (God in God's self).

   3. The pseudepigraphic work of the Kohen brothers of Castile developed a connection of evil to demons and an understanding of the Messiah in terms of a battle with evil.

IV. Another form of Kabbalism, associated with Rabbi Abraham Abulafia (1240–c.1291), is Prophetic Kabbalism.

A. In contrast to the tight circles of scholars who focused on the esoteric study of Torah, Abulafia lived an active, itinerant life and produced both speculative and ecstatic (prophetic) writings.

   1. Born in Saragossa, he traveled to the Near East, Greece, and Spain.

   2. He had a strong messianic consciousness and, in 1280, traveled to Rome and confronted Pope Nicholas III in the hope of bringing on the Messianic Age.

   3. An admirer of Maimonides, Rabbi Abulafia wrote a mystical supplement to that philosopher's work and considered his Kabbalism to be a combination of Maimonides and the *Book of Creation*.

B. Rabbi Abulafia's words of encouragement to his followers reveal his form of Prophetic Mysticism.

    1. Prophesy, he says, is an expression of the love of God. Objections his followers might raise to the mystical path are representations of an "evil inclination" that will "seduce you to die without wisdom, understanding, and the knowledge of God."

    2. For Abulafia, this form of mysticism is not optional. It is a way of participating in the life of the world to come.

C. Abulafia's writings contain practical directions for the achievement of ecstasy, what he called the "loosening of the knots."

    1. Without using the technical language concerning *sefirot*, he shared the perception of Scripture as a web of divine significance in every letter and number.

    2. Psychic release is accomplished through speaking, writing, and recombining words, letters, and numbers. The mind is released through concentration and associative leaps.

Recommended Reading:

Dan, J., ed., *The Early Kabbalah*.

Questions to Consider:

1. What logically follows from the premise that the words of Torah form a world that one might inhabit?

2. Discuss the implications of the practice of gematria: assigning numerical values to letters of the alphabet.

Lecture Seven—Transcript
The Beginnings of Kabbalah

The devout of Germany, the *Hasidei Ashkenazi*, were not simply a stepping stone toward Kabbalism; they formed a sort of piety that still thrives among many Jews. Yet they were also something of a stepping stone; elements within the German Hasidism continue on in other forms of Jewish Mysticism. In this presentation, we begin to trace the development of the form of mysticism that is most identified with Judaism, quite properly, and has had a remarkable longevity, extending down to the present. We take up the beginnings of Kabbalah.

The complexity and creativity that characterized medieval Judaism was partly due to external challenges and partly due to internal factors. We saw, in the previous lecture, how the *Hasidei Ashkenazi* can be seen, in part, as a response to the threat of Christian oppression that kept Jews on the margins of society and, in part, as integrating Christian themes, such as its emphasis on repentance. Certainly, any consideration of this medieval Jewish life must also take into account the internal factor of Moses Maimonides, Moses ben Maimon (or, using the tradition's internal method of acronyms, Rambam), whose dates are 1135–1204. He himself had mystical tendencies, but he is renowned fundamentally as somebody who heroically sought to preserve the truth, the integrity, and the vibrancy of Judaism in response to the intellectual challenges of Muslim philosophy. This is one of the external factors to which Moses Maimonides responded from within. This challenge of Islamic philosophy is represented by figures known in Latin as Avicenna and Averroës; we will meet them in their Arabic guise later, in Unit 3.

Maimonides responded in the manner of the Christian thinker Thomas Aquinas, taking on the best of this Islamic philosophy that was deeply influenced by Aristotle and trying to come to grips with it from within the framework of his Jewish faith. He was a prodigy of learning in law, medicine, and philosophy. He wrote a book called *The Luminary*, which is a commentary on the Mishnah. He wrote another book called *The Eight Chapters*, which is a commentary on a single book in the Mishnah, namely, the "Sayings of the Fathers." And he wrote two other things which are deeply controversial. One of them is called Mishnah Torah; that is a codification of the Torah. This upset many Rabbinic Jews, because the whole nature of the

Talmudic tradition was that it was ever expanding without strict codification. Maimonides's attempt to make it neat and tidy was resisted by some Jews, as was his writing *The Thirteen Principles*, the first effort to really construct a Jewish frame of belief or creeds, 13 propositions; it clearly resembled much too much the Christian creed. And the nature of Judaism had always been less what one believes than what one did and the observance of the Commandments of Torah. These elements in Maimonides's response to the intellectual currents pushed from Christianity on one side and Islam on the other side made him a very controversial figure, and some Jews attacked Maimonides and did not accept his position as a representative of Judaism, but others defended him.

Noteworthy among his defenders is a Jewish scholar named Nachmonides in the Latin version (or Moses ben Nachman Gerondi), who was, again, deeply learned in Talmud, medicine, and philosophy and one of the key developers of the Kabbalistic tradition, deeply committed to mysticism. He saw that Maimonides's intentions were profoundly good. He did not agree with Maimonides's positions, but he defended him against other Jewish teachers and sought to create a compromise position between Maimonides and other Jewish scholars (with very little success, it should be said). The book that Maimonides wrote that had the biggest influence, however, on the mystical tradition was his book called the *Guide of the Perplexed*, which tried to work out a defense for Jewish belief and Jewish practice in light of these intellectual currents. We will see, as we progress in our survey of Kabbalism, how various scholars know and respond to Maimonides. Although he is not a mystic himself, he has a real impact on these subsequent mystics.

The earliest stages of Kabbalism reveal an intense desire to respect the past—the term Kabbalah means, simply, "tradition." But that respect for the past is combined with an intense creativity, which I think is generated by the socio-religious context, the concentration of imagination in small groups of Jewish scholars working at the Talmud, interpreting the Torah, in small towns in Provence and Spain. Although the 13th-century composition called the *Zohar* is correctly regarded as the normative text of this tradition, and we will take it up explicitly in the next lecture, it was preceded by at least a century of spectacular developments in mysticism. It is possible that there is some cross-influence between Christian dualistic movements, such as the Albigensians and the Cathars, and the development of Jewish Kabbalism. These Christian groups had a very strong dualism. They tended to think in terms of divine emanations, and so it is possible that early Kabbalists had some influence from them, but it's not really necessary to posit such influence. They were in the area. The Albigensians were in the same area of Provence and Spain, but it's better, perhaps, to think of Kabbalism as rising from within the Jewish tradition, because all of the elements were there already in movements like Merkabah Mysticism.

What is important for understanding early Kabbalism are the assumptions and antecedents to the 12th-century developments, and I'm going to spend a moment on this, because I think if we grasp these assumptions, the subsequent permutations will be much better understood. The fundamental assumptions concern the way God is present in the world and the human means of engaging that presence. I've said from the beginning that mysticism is about the effort to contact God, to engage God directly, rather than through mediation. So the questions of how God is in the world and how humans engage God's presence in the world are critical.

The first assumption concerns Torah, the very text of Scripture. For these Jews in the medieval period, Torah is not only a text that speaks about God; it is God speaking. It is not simply a text that speaks about the world; the inspired word of God *is* the world. And here, I think it is important for us to imagine small groups of men sitting around a Torah scroll in a dimly lit room with a few candles shining, studying these ancient hieroglyphs in the text, and in some sense, they really are inhabiting that world. It is not simply that they can imagine the world that the Bible imagines; what they imagine is, in fact, in the room with them. I think this is really important. The Torah creates a world that they inhabit.

Secondly, this Torah world, the inspired Scripture, contains something of God in every word, every individual word and every individual letter, in every part of a letter; everything reveals God at some level, because it is God speaking. God's word is quite literally in that text; everything has meaning, and that meaning has been teased out, remember, over almost 1,000 years now of scholars studying every consonant, every vowel marking, every syllable, asking of themselves and each other: Why does the text say this and not that? What does God want to get through to us through putting the words together in this fashion? The third assumption is that words and letters have significance numerically, as well as semantically. I touched on this in the previous lecture when I spoke about the practice of gematria. I mentioned that in languages in which the letters of the alphabet serve also as the numbers, combinations of numbers create words, and the letters of the words also create numbers, thus enabling the mystical exchanges of numbers and words.

Fourth, there is a mystical connection between the world of Scripture and the human person. God reveals God's self in the text of Torah, but also the human person is created in the image of God, so there is some correspondence between God in the text and the image of God in the human person who studies the text. We have God, we have the human being, and the place of meeting is Torah. God is in the Torah, the humans inhabit the Torah, and therefore, we have this mutual presence of God and humans found in the study of Torah. Some of the earlier mystical tradition in Judaism anticipated later developments. In Merkabah Mysticism, I mentioned how there was the practice called *Shiur Koma*, the "measure of the body," literally. This was speculation on God in all of God's transcendence in terms of a human body. There was speculation about the limbs of God, and these limbs are described in terms of absolutely gigantic numbers. You'll remember that we read a text which spoke of a 500-year journey from one stage of heaven to another stage of heaven. Similarly, with the body of God, there is this effort to, number one, express God's immanence by imagining God in terms of the human body, and yet because that cosmic body is so enormous, also to emphasize God's otherness and God's distance from humans.

A second preparation for what we find in Kabbalism is a very short work whose date is unknown—but it certainly existed before the 10th century—known as the *Book of Creation, Sefer Yesirah*. This book, for the first time, speaks of emanations from God and uses the term *sefirot*, which will become a technical word in Kabbalism and a key word in this form of mysticism. The *sefirot* should be imagined as rays, as from light or emanations. It is, if you will, God extending God's self into the world. This is already there in the *Book of Creation* by the 10th century.

I turn to the first manifestations of Kabbalah in Provence and Spain, which reveal the work of many scholars in a cooperative effort. The first book that clearly marks the beginning of Kabbalah is called *Sefer ha-Bahir, The Book of Brilliance*. It is an anonymous work of the 12th century that has pivotal significance. First, it uses the ancient style of midrash on Scripture to communicate its new ideas. We've seen earlier that apocalyptic literature used pseudonymous authorship in order to appear as though it has been written many years prior to the time of its actual composition. Here, we find an author imitating an ancient style of composition. He interprets Scripture using the sort of midrashic style that was used by the ancient rabbinic scholars. There is this sense of: "Here's Kabbalah, you see, it's tradition." It's not new or innovative. It is coming from the past, and yet it introduces new ideas. Innovation is slipped in through the camouflage of an ancient garment.

The book introduces the notion of a female component in the divinity for the first time, using the symbol that we saw among the *Hasidei Ashkenazi* of the Shekinah, the divine presence. And since that is female in Hebrew, it is now beginning to be possible to think of a sort of duality in God—a male principle, a female principle. You'll notice that this represents something of a gendering of God, which will correspond to the gendered character of the human person. The *Sefer ha-Bahir* speculates on the workings of evil, connecting evil especially to material reality. Here, we see something of the dualism that we would find among the Albigensians, for example. And it begins to organize the *sefirot* that had first been mentioned in the *Book of Creation*. *Sefer ha-Bahir* really gives attention to the *sefirot*, makes them 10 in number and studies them in considerable detail. This is a section, 124, from the *Sefer ha-Bahir*. It takes its point of origin from the blessing of Aaron. When Aaron blesses the people, he holds up his hands, and if we look at my hands, we see that I have 10 fingers raised. And so the question is asked:

> And what is the reason for the raising of the hands and blessing them with the benediction? This is because there are 10 fingers on the hands, a hint to the 10 *sefirot* by which the sky and the earth were sealed. And those 10 correspond to the 10 commandments, and within these 10 all 613 *mitzvoth* [or commandments] are included. If you count the number of letters of the 10 commandments you will find that there are 613 letters, comprising all 22 letters of the alphabet, except for the letter *tet*, which is absent. What is the reason for this?

> To teach you that the *tet* represents *beTen* (stomach, abdomen), and not the *sefirot*.

Let me give you a warning right now: This stuff is highly technical. You can't learn Kabbalah on the Internet or by signing up for a certificate of study in Kabbalah. It requires initiation. It requires knowledge of Hebrew. It requires the close study of these texts, and it takes a great deal of time. For people like us who are approaching from outside, what strikes us mainly is how arcane this is, how odd this is, how without point all of this is. Again, I invite you to remember small groups of men sitting around this text. This is the world in which they are, through such questions, coming into contact with the presence of God, God's Shekinah.

Section 125 says, "And why are they called *sefirot*?" And the answer is given in terms of a scriptural citation from Psalm 19:2, because it is written: "The heavens declare (*mesaprim*) the Glory (*kavod*) of God." Now, this is nonsense. This is not the etymology of the word *sefirot*, which is simply not a scriptural word, but everything must be found in Scripture. So this "close-enough" etymology, *mesaprim*, sounds just enough like *sefirot* to be the scriptural warrant for using this term, especially when it's combined with the sense of God's *kavod*, or glory, which we saw among the *Hasidei Ashkenazi* was one of the ways in which God's immanence was communicated. That's the *Sefer ha-Bahir*. It's very obscure, very learned, deeply engaged in Scripture—and for those who are not initiated, deeply puzzling.

Other scholars also made important contributions to this developing form of mysticism. Rabbi Isaac the Blind contributed further speculation on the *sefirot*, creating a panoramic understanding of God and the world, and the possibility—and this is important—of union, *devequt,* through Kabbalistic study, so that it is the mystical study of the text that brings God and humans together. You have God and Torah, humans and Torah; God and humans meet in Torah. The Gerona circle in Catalonia includes the author I mentioned earlier in this lecture, Moses ben Nachman, and Rabbi Azriel, who expounded the relationship between the *sefirot*, the emanations, and another term, the *Eyn Sof*. The *sefirot* are emanations from the divine into the world. The *Eyn Sof* is the term for God in God's self. So, Rabbi Azriel of Gerona asks:

If a questioner asks: Who can compel me to believe in *Eyn Sof*? Answer: Know that everything visible and perceivable to human contemplation is limited, and that everything that is limited is finite, and that everything that is finite is insignificant. Conversely, that which is not limited is called *Eyn Sof* and is absolutely undifferentiated in a complete and changeless unity. And if He is without limit, then nothing exists outside him. And since He is both exalted and hidden, He is the essence of all that is concealed and revealed.

This goes beyond paradox, but you see that what is happening here is the attempt to bring together both God's transcendence, the *Eyn Sof* (God is other; God is holy; God cannot be known in Godself), and God's immanence (God can be known in God's emanations, in the rays that come from God and are perceivable in creation).

Finally, the Kohen brothers of Castile also use pseudepigraphy in their works (we will find this again in the *Zohar*) and develop a connection of evil to demons and an understanding of the Messiah in terms of a battle with evil. This is a very important contribution by the Kohen brothers, because we will see that there is now—in contrast to the *Hasidei Ashkenazi*, who said, "Don't think about the Messiah at all; nobody can know about the Messiah,"—we find that messianic thought is finding its way back into Kabbalism. And we will see that in the stage after the *Zohar*; when we turn to Lurianic Kabbalism, we will see that Messianism as a cosmic battle against evil is very much again with us.

There is, finally, another form of Kabbalism that is associated with Rabbi Abulafia, whose dates are 1240–c. 1291. His name is Abraham Abulafia. Following Gershom Scholem, I identify his form of Kabbalism as Prophetic Kabbalism. In contrast to the tight circles of scholars who focused on the esoteric study of Torah, Abulafia lived an active, itinerant life and produced both speculative and ecstatic (what he called "prophetic") writings. He was born in Saragossa in Spain. He traveled to the Near East, and then Greece, and then back to Spain. He clearly had a very strong messianic consciousness in connection with himself, because in 1280, he traveled to Rome and confronted Pope Nicholas III in the hope of bringing on the Messianic Age. He was an admirer of Maimonides, and he wrote a mystical supplement to that philosopher's work. He considered his Kabbalism to be something of a combination of

Maimonides on one side and the *Book of Creation* on the other. I would like to begin with Abulafia with some of his words of encouragement to his followers on following this form of Prophetic Mysticism. He says:

> Prophecy is a mode of the intellect. It is the expression of the love of the Lord our God, the Lord is One. It is well known that those who love prophecy love God and they are beloved of God. Undoubtedly these are called sages and prophets. Observe and realize that the numerical value of the word "lovers" (*'ohavim*) is the same as that of the word "prophecy" (*nevu'ah*) [we see how gematria works here; prophecy and lovers go together] and by "lovers" I mean "beloved prophets." This stage of prophecy is itself the worship of God in love.

And then he deals with all of the objections that his follower might have: It takes so long; it's so difficult; I'm not worthy.

> There is also the hindrance caused by exile in which a man is like a slave sold to those who force him to toil in order to make bricks and mortar. And there are many other similar hindrances. [But then he assures his student.] But, my son, I swear to you that all these are excuses made by that harsh evil inclination which engages in battle in order to seduce you to die without wisdom, understanding, and the knowledge of God, soiling you with bricks and mortar so that no portion in the World to Come be given you.

For Abraham Abulafia, this form of mysticism is not optional. It is a way of participating in the life of the world to come. His writings contain practical directions for the achievement of ecstasy, what Abulafia calls the "loosening of the knots," the loosening of the psychic bonds that constrain us through rational thought. Without sharing the technical language concerning *sefirot*, he shared the perception of Scripture as a web of divine significance in every letter and every number. And so he instructs his follower on how to accomplish psychic release through the speaking and writing of words, letters, and numbers, and their recombinations. The mind is released through concentration and associative leaps.

> Be prepared for thy God, O Israelite! Make thyself ready to direct thy heart to God alone. Cleanse the body and choose a

lonely house where none shall hear thy voice. Sit there in thy closet and do not reveal thy secret to any man. If thou canst, do it by day in the house, but it is best if thou completest it during the night. In the hour when thou preparest thyself to speak with the Creator, if thou wishest Him to reveal His might to thee, then be careful to abstract all thy thought from the vanities of this world. Cover thyself with thy prayer shawl and put *tefillin* on thy head and hands that thou mayest be filled with awe of the *Shekinah* which is near thee [the divine presence]. ... If it be night, kindle many lights, until all be bright. Then take ink, pen, and a table to thy hand and remember that thou art about to serve God in the joy of the gladness of heart. Now begin to combine a few or many letters, to permute and combine them until thy heart be warm. Then be mindful of their movements and of what thou canst bring forth by moving them. And when thou feelest that thy heart is already warm and when thou seest that by combinations of letter thou can grasp new things which by human tradition or by thyself that wouldst not be able to know and when thou art thus prepared to receive the influx of divine power which flows into thee, then turn all thy true thought to imagine His name and His exalted angels in thy heart as if they were human beings sitting or standing about. Thy whole body [at this point] will be seized by an extremely strong trembling, so that thou wilt think that truly thou art about to die, because thy soul, overjoyed with its knowledge, will leave thy body. [Be ready to die at that moment of ecstasy.] Then, [when it's over] return to the matters of the body, rise and eat and drink a little, or refresh thyself with a pleasant odor, and restore thy spirit to its sheath until another time, and rejoice at thy lot and know that God loveth thee!

This is a remarkably valuable firsthand witness to the technique used to accomplish mystical ecstasy on the basis of Torah. In this session, we've only been able to touch on some dimensions of the Kabbalah. In the next lecture, we will consider its mature form in the *Zohar*, the *Book of Splendor*.

Lecture Eight
Mature Kabbalah—*Zohar*

Scope:

For the Jewish practitioners of Kabbalah, the *Zohar* (*Book of Splendor*) has a status next to that held by Torah and Talmud. Presenting itself as "tradition" (Kabbalah) from the period of the early rabbis, the *Zohar* is actually the astonishing literary creation of a Spanish Jewish mystic, Moses de León, between the years 1275–1286. This lecture takes up the fascinating tale of the *Zohar*'s production, describes the discrete parts of this massive composition, provides a sample of its language (in translation), and offers a brief sketch of its vision of God and the world and the place of humans within God's creation.

Outline

I. This lecture looks at mature Kabbalah as expressed in the *Book of Splendor*, the *Zohar*. Like some of its Kabbalistic predecessors, the *Zohar*, the canonical text of Jewish Mysticism, hides its origin in a specific time and author.

  A. The *Sefer ha-Bahir* and the works of the Kohen brothers imitated the style of ancient midrash and were ascribed to earlier authors.

  B. The *Zohar* presents itself as a work from the age of the Tannaim (the first generation of rabbinic teachers), especially Simeon ben Yohai; this attribution is still accepted by many orthodox Kabbalists.

   1. In the *Zohar*, the sage Simeon ben Yohai wanders Palestine with his son and his disciples, but it is a fictional Palestine.

   2. He discourses on Scripture in the style of midrash in Aramaic, but it is an artificial Aramaic.

  C. Critical scholarship, particularly that of Gershom Scholem, has established that the author of the *Zohar* was a Spanish Jew named Moses de León (d. 1305).

   1. León studied Maimonides in 1264 but also immersed himself in classical sources (Torah, Talmud) and earlier Kabbalistic literature.

2. In the city of Guadalajara from 1275–1280, he began to produce a mystical midrash concerning parts of Torah and the book of Ruth. Then, he began to distribute his commentaries but not as his own work.

3. Between 1280 and 1286, León wrote the remainder of the *Zohar*, a commentary on Torah consisting of a number of discrete compositions.

4. From 1286 to his death in 1305, he composed a rather large number of other writings in his own name while continuing to distribute copies of the *Zohar*.

II. Analysis of the *Zohar* reveals some of its complexity and distinctive character.

A. It is a work of great length (in Aramaic, more than 2,400 printed pages), and only relatively small portions have been translated into English.

B. It is made up of 22 distinct compositions, plus a few scattered fragments.

1. Several significant compositions take the form of commentaries on Torah, such as the lengthy untitled opening section, the *Sifra di-Tseniutha* (*Book of Conciliation*), and the *Sithre Torah* (*Secrets of the Torah*).

2. Also included are romantic tales, such as "The Old Man" and "The Child," that contain mystical teachings on Torah, the soul, and prayer.

3. Treatises on traditional subjects of mysticism, including the *Hekhaloth*, "Palaces"; *Raza de-Razin*, "Secret of Secrets"; and *Sithre Othioth*, "Secrets of the Letters," also find a place in the compilation.

4. It's important to note that mystics find mysticism wherever they look; in other words, the mystical character of texts is not determined by their subject matter but by the manner in which they are read. The parts of the *Zohar* that appear to be ordinary and down to earth can be as powerfully mystical to their readers as those parts that seem to be strange.

C. In contrast to the ecstatic or Prophetic Kabbalism of Abraham Abulafia, the *Zohar* is scholarly rather than popular.

    1. The length and complexity of the work resist easy or quick appropriation.

    2. The complex symbolic language creates its own world and requires initiation.

    3. The doctrine (theosophy) of the composition is indirect, clothed by simple-appearing tales, sayings, and comments.

D. Two passages from the *Zohar* provide a taste of its style and sensibility, even in English translation.

    1. "How to Look at Torah" offers a glimpse at the esoteric presuppositions of Kabbalistic reading.

    2. "Male and Female" illustrates the *Zohar*'s strong sense of gender and sexual complementarity.

III. The *Zohar* is not a practical manual on how to practice mysticism but, rather, expresses a theosophy, an understanding of God and world. This theosophy is expressed indirectly, through the reading of Torah.

A. In agreement with earlier Kabbalah, the *Zohar*'s understanding of God is at once transcendent and immanent.

    1. God in Godself (*Eyn Sof*) is utterly unknowable and can be approached only through negation.

    2. God in the world, in Torah, is in humans through these divine emanations.

B. In the *Zohar*, the system of *sefirot* is at once systematic and dynamic; each *sefirah* can be diagrammed spatially.

    1. At the top is *keter* ("the crown"), which is equivalent to *Eyn Sof* and is without differentiation; through it comes hokhmah ("wisdom"). The third of the *sefirot* is *binah* ("womb").

    2. In this triad—*keter*, hokhmah, and *binah*—hokhmah is male, and *binah* is female. *Binah* receives the seed of hokhmah, and they conceive the seven lower *sefirot*.

    3. *Binah* gives birth, first, to *din* ("judgment"), also called *gevurah* ("power"), and, then, to *chesed* ("mercy"); they are the left and right arms or hands of God. Their balance is symbolized by the central *siferah*, namely, *tif'eret* ("balance") or *rachamim* ("compassion"). If *din* is overemphasized, the results are imbalance and evil. *Tif'eret* is the trunk of the divine body.

4. *Nezah* ("endurance") and *hod* ("majesty") are the right and left legs of the body, corresponding to Moses and Aaron. *Yesod* ("foundation") is the phallus, symbolizing the procreative power of creation.

5. The final *sefirah* is called most often Shekinah ("presence") or *malkuth* ("kingdom"). Ideally, this is where Israel dwells.

C. The flexibility of this system is found in two factors: First, the *sefirot* represent dynamic forces and enter into diverse combinations. Second, each of the *sefirah* uses a biblical word, so that when we read the Bible, we will constantly discover God's self-revelation.

IV. Corresponding to this theosophy is a distinct understanding of the human situation and vocation.

A. Humans are created in the image of God, and ideally, the divine *sefirot* are also found in humans.

B. Just as imbalance among the *sefirot* introduces evil into the cosmos, so does an imbalance within humans, causing the separation of what should be united. This understanding is found in the concept of *tikkun ha-olam* ("mending the world").

1. By keeping the Commandments of God, each individual Jew and Israel as a whole work to mend the world.

2. The constant study of Torah as the body of God enables the mystical adherence to God (*devequt*) but also accomplishes in the life of the mystic what the cosmos still lacks.

C. Given the sexual symbolism of the system, marriage is highly valued as a symbol of divine marriage; Sabbath Eve is the weekly celebration of the sacred wedding and the ideal time for mystics to make love.

Recommended Reading:

Scholem, G. *Origins of the Kabbalah.*

Questions to Consider:

1. Discuss how the *sefirot* help mystics grasp the tension between the otherness of God and God's immanence.

2. In what manner does Kabbalah provide a sense of cosmic mission for the practice of mysticism?

Lecture Eight—Transcript
Mature Kabbalah—*Zohar*

We have sketched the beginnings of the major form of Jewish Mysticism called Kabbalah in the activities of small groups of mystics in Provence and Spain and in the prophetic Kabbalism of Abraham of Abulafia. two distinct approaches: one deeply theosophical, a form of gnosis with an emphasis on the analysis of the divine realm, the *Eyn Sof*, and the *sefirot*; the other profoundly practical, showing how the combination and recombination of words and letters and their numerical significance could unloose the knots of psychic constraint and lead to states of ecstasy. Yet both forms of insipient Kabbalism are joined by a devotion to the world of Torah. In this presentation, I consider mature Kabbalah as expressed in the *Book of Splendor*, the *Zohar*.

Like some of its Kabbalistic predecessors, the *Zohar*—the *Book of Splendor*—which is the canonical text of Jewish Mysticism and, for Jewish mystics, holds the place of the Torah and the midrash for the exoteric tradition, hides its specific place of origin in terms of time and author. It hides behind the cloak of antiquity. We have seen how, in apocalyptic literature, the device of pseudonymity was used to try to convince readers that what was being said by a contemporary was actually said by an ancient figure, such as Enoch. And we saw in the *Sefer ha-Bahir—The Book of Brilliance*—and in the works of the Kohen brothers the use of midrash, the style of midrash, to make readers feel as though they were engaging ancient forms of writing rather than contemporary forms of writing. The *Zohar* does much the sort of same thing: introduces innovation as though it were ancient and, thus, capitalizes on the very term Kabbalah, which means "tradition." The *Zohar* presents itself as coming from the age of the Tannaim. The Tannaim are the very first generations of rabbinic teachers from before the year 200, people like Rabbi Akiva, Johanan ben Zakkai, and others. It presents itself as though it were this ancient writing, specifically writings about a 1st-century *tanna* called Simeon ben Yohai. And this attribution is still accepted by many orthodox Kabbalists; they regard it as precisely such an ancient work. If one accepts that ancient attribution, one can understand why the *Zohar* is given such astonishing prestige, because it would seem to derive from exactly the same period, or perhaps even before, the Mishnah and the Talmud and, thus, lay a particular claim upon

Jewish life: It makes mysticism begin when Judaism began. We have seen in the course of these lectures that, in fact, that conviction is right; mysticism did begin when Judaism began, but the *Zohar* was not there when Judaism began.

We see in the *Zohar* that the sage Simeon ben Yohai wanders Palestine with his son and his disciples, but it is a fictional Palestine. It doesn't reflect actual local knowledge. He discourses on Scripture in the style of midrash in Aramaic, but it is an artificial Aramaic. It is not semantically the same language that was spoken in ancient Palestine. Critical scholarship, especially that of Gershom Scholem, has investigated the *Zohar* using the tools of critical historiography and has established that the author was a very specific person, a Spanish Jew named Moses de León, who died in 1305. Moses de León is a figure about whom we know a few things: He studied Maimonides in 1264 but was also interested in the classical sources—Torah and Talmud (he actually knew midrash; he actually knew Talmud), and he was deeply fascinated by earlier Kabbalistic literature, such as the *Sefer ha-Bahir*, *The Book of Brilliance*. In the city of Guadalajara, between the years of 1275–1280, Moses de León began to produce a mystical midrash on parts of Torah, the first five books of Moses, and the book of Ruth. And fascinatingly, after he finishes this, he begins to distribute it to other scholars and to interested parties but not as his own work. He begins to distribute it as something that he found, that he discovered. He begins the process by which his own work is covered by means of this fictional guise of antiquity.

Then, between the years 1280–1286, he wrote the remainder of the *Zohar*. It is quite an astonishing literary production, which forms a commentary on Torah consisting in a number of discrete compositions, which I will describe in a moment. Fascinatingly, from that period when he finished the *Zohar* until his death in the year 1305, he composed a rather large number of other writings in his own name while continuing to distribute copies of the *Zohar* as though it came from antiquity. This is a rather fascinating process of dissemination, and even then, not everybody accepted it as authentically ancient. But because he wrote works in his own name, he could more convincingly argue that this particular work had been discovered by him, had simply come to him. He wasn't its author; he was only its distributor. So the *Zohar* begins to affect and be read by those Kabbalists not as a recent work but as an astonishingly large and powerful work that comes from the heart of antiquity.

Analysis of the *Zohar* reveals some of its complexity and distinctive character. The first thing that we need to be aware of is that it is huge. It is a work of great length. In Aramaic, it is over 2,400 printed pages, and only relatively small portions of it have ever been translated into English. So folks who claim to have read the *Zohar* who don't know Aramaic have not. Furthermore, one can only properly do Kabbalah with the *Zohar* on the basis of the Aramaic text. All of the word plays, all of the numerical values, all of the gematria that we have spoken about, the plays on words and letters and numbers—all of this is possible only in the original language. It becomes unintelligible when one translates it over to other languages. It is an enormous work and a work that is daunting, and only portions of which have been available to readers such as you and me. The *Zohar* is made up of 22 distinct compositions, so like the Bible, it is rather more of an anthology of works than a single literary work from beginning to end. It is, in a sense, several distinct compositions and then a number of scattered fragments—not even complete compositions—that are inserted. Several of the large compositions take the form of commentaries on Torah. For example, the very long opening section of the *Zohar* is a sustained commentary on the Torah. In addition, the *Sifra di-Tseniutha*, the *Book of Conciliation*, and the *Sithre Torah*, the *Secrets of the Torah*, also take the form of line-by-line commentaries on the scriptural text.

But in addition to the Torah commentary, there are romantic tales, short stories, such as "The Old Man" and "The Child," that contain mystical teachings on Torah, the soul, and prayer. Please remember this when we come to Hasidic Judaism later in this unit, where storytelling becomes such an important indirect way of teaching mysticism. We find precedent for that already here in the *Zohar*. And then the *Zohar* contains mystical treatises on traditional subjects of mysticism: the *Hekaloth*, the "Palaces"; the *Raza de-Razin*, the "Secret of Secrets"; the *Sithre Othioth*, the "Secrets of the Letters"; elements of Merkabah Mysticism. In a sense, it is an anthology of virtually all mystical impulses in Judaism up to this time.

I would like to remind you, or perhaps alert you for the first time to, the realization that within small groups of readers that think of themselves as mystics and who are practicing mysticism, the mystical character of texts doesn't rely on their subject matter, or even their language, or the fact that they are esoteric and difficult to read. Mystics find mysticism wherever they look, so a text—a short story like "The Old Man," a short story like "The Child"—can yield mystical meaning in the same way as the story of Moses ascending the mountain. It's not the subject matter that makes it mystical; it's the mystic's eyes that make it mystical. The parts of the *Zohar* that appear to be very ordinary and down to earth can be as powerfully mystical for the readers of the *Zohar* as those parts that seem to be "oogy-boogy" and very strange.

In contrast to the ecstatic or Prophetic Kabbalism of Abraham Abulafia, the *Zohar* is scholarly rather than popular. The length and complexity of the work resist easy or quick appropriation. You can't do a quick-fix Kabbalism. The complex symbolic language creates its own world and requires initiation. The meaning of the *Zohar*, in other words, does not lie out there on the surface. It is not exoteric. One must become a member of the group that reads in this way in order properly to appreciate it, so that the doctrine, or the theosophy, the vision of reality, that is found in the *Zohar* is not self-evident; it is indirect. It is clothed, in fact, by astonishingly simple-appearing tales, and sayings, and comments.

I would like to read two passages from the *Zohar* which I think are relatively accessible, and they provide a sense of its style and its sensibility, even in English translation. The first section is entitled, by its English translator, "How to Look at Torah." And I think this, in some sense, summarizes a great deal of what I've been saying in the last several lectures.

> Rabbi Shim'on said, "Woe to the human being who says that Torah presents mere stories and ordinary words! If so, we could compose a Torah right now with ordinary words and better than all of them! To present matters of the world? Even rulers of the world possess words more sublime. If so, let us follow them and make a Torah out of them! Ah, the words of Torah are sublime words, sublime secrets!

And then he develops this image that angels, who are spirits, must take on bodies when they come into the world in order to appear to humans. In the same way, God's word, Torah, must take on clothing when it comes into the world. He says:

If this is so with angels, how much more so with Torah who created them and all the worlds and for whose sake they all exist! In descending to this world, if she did not put on the garments of this world, the world could not endure.

In other words, Torah is so great that the world would disappear and be destroyed if it weren't clothed.

So this story of Torah is the garment of Torah. Whoever thinks that the garment is the real Torah and not something else—may his spirit deflate! He will have no portion in the world that is coming. Come and see: There is a garment visible to all. When those fools see someone in a good-looking garment, they look no further. But the essence of the garment is the body; The essence of the body is the soul!

You have to keep on going deeper. Don't stop at the garment; go to the body. Don't stop at the body; go for the soul. We're working from the exoteric to the esoteric. "So it is with Torah. She has a body: the commandments of Torah." Notice he's making a distinction now between the stories of Torah and the Commandments. The stories are the garment. The Commandments are the body. This is called the "embodiment of Torah." The *Zohar* says:

This body is clothed in garments: the stories of this world. Fools of the world look only at that garment, the story of Torah; they know nothing more. They do not look at what is under that garment. Those who know more do not look at the garment but rather at the body under that garment. The wise ones, servants of the King on high, those who stood at Mount Sinai, look only at the soul, the root of all, real Torah! In the time to come they are destined to look at the soul of the soul of Torah!

It's not the stories; it's not the Commandments; it's the inner meaning of the Commandments which is the inner soul of Torah. "Come and see," the *Zohar* says.

So it is above. There is garment and body and soul and soul of soul. The heavens and their host are the garment. The Communion of Israel is the body who receives the soul, the Beauty of Israel. So She is the body of the soul. The soul we have mentioned is the beauty of Israel who is real Torah.

The soul of the soul is the Holy Ancient One. So, the soul within the soul is God. "All is connected. This one to that one," which is the point I was trying to make in a previous lecture. God, Torah, the human person—all are connected.

> Woe to the wicked who say that Torah is merely a story! They look at this garment and no further. Happy are the righteous who look at Torah properly! [This concludes with a final simile.] "As wine must sit in a jar, so Torah must in this garment! So look only at what is under the garment! So all those words and all those stories—they are garments!

I think this wonderfully expressed the mystics' conviction that the outward form of Scripture is less important than the inward commandment. And the commandment is even less important than the transformation of the individual soul in the presence of God. Another short passage, called "Male and Female" by the translator, illustrates, I think, the *Zohar's* very strong sense of gender, and I'll return to this point. Male and female are very, very important in this mysticism. Rabbi Shim'on said:

> High mysteries are revealed in these two verses, "Male and female He created them" to make known the Glory on high, the mystery of faith. Out of this mystery Adam was created. Male and female He created them. From here we learn: Any image that does not embrace [the] male and [the] female is not a high and true image. We have established this in the mystery of our Mishnah. Come and see: The Blessed Holy One does not place His abode in any place where male and female are not found together. Blessings are found only in a place where male and female are found, as it is written: He blessed them and called their name Adam on the day that they were created. It is not written: He blessed him and called his name Adam. A human being is only called Adam when male and female are as one.

There is a strong sense of gender complementarity—male and female go together as forming the full human. And since the human corresponds to the divine, we are also going to have male/female elements in speculation about the divine. Now the *Zohar*, it should be clear at this point, is not a practical manual on how to practice mysticism. This is not Abraham of Abulafia, who tells you to go to your closet with your pen and ink and start scrambling letters. This is a theosophy, an understanding, a vision of creation, of God and the world. But it does it indirectly, through the reading of Torah. It doesn't say, "Here's how the world looks." It basically says, "Here's what Torah is saying," and the grid of its understanding is one that is learned through initiation, rather than directly in the text. In agreement with earlier Kabbalah, its understanding of God is at once transcendent and immanent. God in Godself, the *Eyn Sof*, is utterly unknowable and can only be approached through negation: God is not this; God is not that. God in the world is knowable and approachable through the *sefirot*, which move immanently through creation. Literally, God is in the world. God is in Torah. God is in humans through these divine emanations.

In the *Zohar*, we get the full system of *sefirot*, which is at once systematic and dynamic. And they can be displayed visually and diagrammatically. I will attempt to lay out these 10 *sefirot* as they are assumed in the *Zohar* to give you a sense of how these emanations are considered. At the very top is *keter*, "the crown." This is equivalent to the *Eyn Sof*; it is the undifferentiated being of God. And from *Eyn Sof* comes hokhmah, "wisdom." The third of the *sefirot* is called *binah*, which means "womb," or "palace," or "understanding." Each of these *sefirot* are given many names. Now we have a triad—the *keter* ("the crown"), hokhmah, and *binah*. Hokhmah is male; *binah* is female. *Binah* receives the seed of hokhmah, and they conceive the seven lower *sefirot*. There is, if you will, spiritual copulation in engendering these further emanations. Notice how the emanations move out of God, out of God in God's self.

Then, *binah* gives birth, first, to *din*, or "judgment" (also called *gevurah*, or "power") and, *chesed*, or "mercy." If *keter*, hokhmah, and *binah* form the head and shoulders of the body of God, *gevurah* and *chesed*, "judgment," or "power," and "mercy," form the left and right arms or hands of God. You see, the *sefirot* are imagined as describing a human body, and so the left hand of God and the right hand of God. Whenever we read in Scripture about God's right hand, we're reading about one of the *sefirot*, one of the emanations, one of the ways in which God is present in creation. When those arms are in balance, they are symbolized by the central emanation, which is called *tif'eret*, "balance," or *rachamim*, "compassion." But when *din* is overemphasized, when judgment is overemphasized, evil results. Notice the origin of evil now is not materiality; it's not demons. It is a disturbance in the divine order. If there's an overemphasis on power, on judgment, rather than compassion, then there is imbalance. When everything is in balance, there is *tif'eret*, which now forms the trunk of the body; so *keter*, hokhmah, *binah*, *gevurah*, *rachamim*, and *tif'eret* is the trunk. *Nezah*, "endurance," and *hod*, ["majesty,"] are equally the right and left legs, which correspond to Moses and Aaron, those biblical figures. The left leg of God and the right leg of God correspond to Moses and Aaron, or majesty and endurance. Hanging from the *tif'eret* is the *yesod*, ["foundation,"] which is the phallus, which symbolizes the procreative power of creation. So we have a complete person here. The final *sefirah* hanging below the *yesod* is called—you're not going to be surprised—most often, Shekinah, that divine presence. Or sometimes, *malkuth*, "kingdom." This is where Israel ideally dwells—in the Shekinah, the presence that is made available through Torah.

The movement downward comes from the *Eyn Sof* into the world, ending in where Israel is, and the way back to God is upward, through those *sefirot*, to *Eyn Sof*. It's quite elaborate but also quite amazingly visual. It is imagining a body of God that reveals itself, in some sense, in the body of the world, the body of Torah, and the body of human beings. The flexibility of this system is found in two factors. First of all, each of these *sefirot*, which I have described as a kind of a diagram of the human body, is not static but dynamic. They can do different things. They can enter into different combinations with different results. The second factor is that each of these *sefirah* uses a biblical word, so that when we're reading the Bible, we are going to constantly be discovering God's self-revelation. When you read *crown*, or *Aaron*, or *Moses*, or *mercy*, or *judgment*, this is not simply a word about the world. This is God in the world. And so it makes the reading of Scripture mystical from beginning to end. Everything reveals the divine emanations.

I understand that this was fairly abstract, but I hope that you get some sense of how this remarkable system works. You don't stand and look at the *sefirot*; rather, the *sefirot* show you how to read, show you how to see reality, show you the way back to God. Corresponding to this theosophy, this vision of reality, is a distinct understanding of the human vocation, the human situation. Humans are created in the image of God, and the divine *sefirot* are ideally found within humans also. Humans also should have balance by having the right proportion between judgment and compassion or power and compassion. Just as the imbalance in the *sefirot* introduces evil into the cosmos, so does an imbalance within humans, causing the separation of what should be united, and so we find this remarkable understanding called *tikkun ha-olam*, "mending the world."

By observing the Commandments of God, by understanding the mysteries of the Commandments of God, each individual Jew and Israel as a whole mends the world. It pulls together the unraveling of the *sefirot* and enables all of the world to respond appropriately to God. In short, the constant study of Torah as the body of God enables the mystical adherence to God, the *devequt*, but also accomplishes in the life of the mystic what the cosmos still lacks. And the work of mysticism, in other words, is not an individualistic indulgence. This is the point we need to end with. It is not an individualistic indulgence; it is a cosmic mission so that what every individual does in obeying God's Commandments has an effect on the entire cosmos.

The final point I want to make, though, is that given the sexual symbolism of this entire system, you will not be surprised to hear that marriage is highly valued as a symbol of the divine marriage. And, indeed, Sabbath Eve—when Jews celebrate the marriage of God and humans in the Sabbath—in the study of Torah, the Sabbath Eve is regarded as the ideal time for mystics to make love so that they have really a hierogamy, a sacred marriage, where husband and wife symbolize the sexual balance that is to be found ideally in the cosmos.

Lecture Nine
Isaac Luria and Safed Spirituality

Scope:

The expulsion of Jews from Spain in 1492 had a profound influence on Jewish Mysticism. Kabbalism went from being confined to small groups to the dominant expression of Judaism, shaped by a more profound sense of loss and exile and incorporating a strong sense of Messianism. The small town of Safed in Galilee became the new center for Kabbalistic teaching, above all, through the influence of the visionary Isaac Luria, and this new form of Kabbalism was spread by Israel Sarug. This lecture considers the important contributions made by the Lurianic school to the Kabbalistic tradition, including the doctrines of *tsimtsum* ("concentration") and *shevirrath ha-kelim* ("breaking of the vessels") and the specific practices involved in *tikkun ha-olam* ("mending the world").

Outline

I. Though the *Zohar* was read as authoritative, Kabbalism was not inflexible. In this lecture, we touch on one of the major developments in this form of mysticism with Isaac Luria and Safed spirituality.

    A. In the 16th and 17th centuries, Kabbalism underwent dramatic changes as a result of external and internal factors.

        1. In Spain and Provence, Kabbalism had flourished among small groups of scholars, but as a result of historical factors, it spread across Judaism in every country.

        2. Externally, the experience of exile under the Catholic emperor of Spain in 1492 forced Jews from their former place of security.

        3. Jews emigrated to lands, such as Egypt and Palestine, that were dominated by Muslim rule rather than Christian and found greater tolerance there.

        4. The small town of Safed in upper Galilee became a new center for Jewish Mysticism; its prestige was enhanced because the Mishnah by Judah ha-Nasi was thought to have been composed there, along with the *Zohar*.

    B. This disruption and relocation encouraged a form of Kabbalism that embraced the realities of history.

1. The theme of transmigration of souls, metempsychosis (in Hebrew, *gilgul*), had existed in earlier Kabbalism, but now the notion of souls leaving one body at death and entering another body could be fused with the notion of the people's exile and restoration.
2. Messianism as the hope for the restoration of the people entered into the mythology of Kabbalism.

II. It was not geography alone that made Safed the new center of Kabbalism but the concurrent presence of three great mystical teachers, two of them also visionaries.

A. Rabbi Joseph ben Ephraim Karo (1488–1575) was a great authority on Jewish Law and author of the *Shulchan Arukh* (the standard code of Law), but he was also a mystic who received revelations about Torah and Kabbalah from his heavenly maggid (messenger or mentor).
1. Extant testimony from a student of Karo, Solomon Alkabetz (c. 1505–1576), gives a firsthand account of one such experience.
2. Karo himself also kept a journal, in which he recorded his mystical experiences.

B. Rabbi Moses ben Jacob Cordovero (1522–1570) was a prolific writer and scholar, whose works include a massive commentary on the *Zohar*.
1. Cordovero was a philosopher of Kabbalah and was concerned with the question of the simultaneous transcendence and immanence of God.
2. For Cordovero, this relationship is stated in the profoundly paradoxical proposition: "God is all reality, but not all reality is God."

C. Isaac Luria (also called Ari, "the Lion," 1534–1572) proved to be the most influential figure in the future shaping of mysticism.
1. He was a scholar but wrote only one book that we know of; his teaching was mainly conveyed through disciples. Luria was a visionary and regarded souls as residing in all things.
2. His most important interpreter was Hayyim Vital (1543–1620), who recorded his own mystical experiences in *Sefer ha-Chezyonot* (the *Book of Visions*).

3. The Lurianic version of Kabbalah was propagated especially by Israel Sarug, who traveled in Europe between 1592–1598, spreading the message.

III. Lurianic Kabbalism shaped the Kabbalistic tradition in a manner that had far-reaching implications.

A. It is perhaps closer to the Prophetic Kabbalism of Abraham Abulafia in its emphasis on personal asceticism and the practice of mysticism. For our study, the term "Practical Mysticism" has two meanings.

1. As might be expected in a group with such visionary experiences, there is an emphasis on the ways of achieving such states, although technique is mostly handed on orally rather than in writing.

2. Practical Kabbalism can also mean theurgy, or magic, the manipulation of symbols in order to bring about certain results. A fascinating aspect of this in Safed spirituality is the practice of phrenology.

B. Three elements of theosophy in particular were developed in Lurianic Mysticism in a more powerfully mythic, even Gnostic direction.

1. *Tsimtsum* ("concentration" or "withdrawal") is the notion that creation becomes possible because of a withdrawal of *Eyn Sof*; creation is real (against Pantheism), but there is an ebb and flow of the *sefirot*, which can be imagined as God's self-exile.

2. *Sherivath ha-Kelim* ("breaking the vessels) is a highly anthropomorphic alignment of the disruption caused by the primordial man (Adam Kadmon) when overwhelmed by the three chief *sefirot* with a disturbing effect on empirical humans: The origin of evil is cosmic disruption and separation.

3. *Tikkun* ("mending" or "uniting") points to the cosmic role of humans. By keeping the Commandments of Torah and by adherence (*devequt*) to the body of Torah through strict intention (*kawwanah*), the mystic helps mend the world.

4. In short, the mystic plays a crucial part in a great cosmic drama of God's self-emptying and return, of rays scattered into creation and gathered again through human effort, of the bringing about of the Messianic Age

through the efforts of faithful Israel and the work of mystics.

IV. Safed spirituality moved Kabbalah into the mainstream of Jewish life everywhere it was practiced.

  A. It made certain ascetical practices, such as fasting, standard for the Jewish community, and Luria's prescriptions for penitents replaced those of the German Hasidim for Jews everywhere.

  B. It contributed a mystical element to the standard Jewish liturgy by the addition of prayers and hymns for individuals and the community.

  C. It provided a unifying vision for Jews everywhere of their participation in the divine drama of loss and redemption.

  D. Even writings of a fundamentally ethical character, such as the *Sheney Luhot ha-Berit* (*The Two Tablets of the Covenant*) by Isaiah ben Abraham Horowitz (1570–1626), were suffused with the sensibility of Lurianic Kabbalah.

  1. A short quotation from Horowitz's *The Generations of Adam* speaks of the relationship between external observance and internal mysticism.

  2. As he continues his work, Horowitz tells readers that he stands in the long tradition of Simeon ben Yohai and his associates, the *Zohar*, and Isaac Luria, but he will add his own thinking to theirs.

Recommended Reading:

Fine, L., trans. and ed., *Safed Spirituality* (*Classics of Western Spirituality.*)

Questions to Consider:

1. Reflect on the notion of "Practical Mysticism" and its theurgic aspects; when does mysticism become "magical thinking"?

2. Consider the impact of external events on the development of mystical movements, taking as an example the Jewish experience of exile from Spain.

Lecture Nine—Transcript
Isaac Luria and Safed Spirituality

The *Book of Splendor*, the *Zohar*, which we discussed in the previous lecture, became canonical for the Jewish mystical tradition. It was read as authoritative, pretty much at the same level as Torah and the Talmud, and as the unquestioned source of wisdom concerning the divine emanations and the human endeavor to heal the world through the practice of the Commandments, the study of God's word, and adherence to mystical truth. This does not mean that Kabbalism became inflexible or did not develop. In this presentation, we touch on one of the major developments with Isaac Luria and Safed spirituality.

In the 16th and 17th centuries, Kabbalism undergoes dramatic changes as a result of external and internal factors. In Spain and Provence, where Kabbalism took its origin, it had flourished in small groups of scholars who gathered around Torah to study it mystically in towns like Gerona. But as a result of these new historical factors, Kabbalism spreads across Judaism in every country. What were those external factors? Primarily, it was the experience of physical exile under the Catholic emperor of Spain in 1492. Jews were physically forced to leave their former place of security, so they experienced actual loss of property, of place, of security. But those same Jews who emigrated to other lands, like Egypt and Palestine, found that they were dominated not by hostile Christians but by far more welcoming Muslim believers, and they found greater tolerance in those lands, so corresponding to exile and loss was also a gain.

The small town in upper Galilee called Safed became the new center for Jewish Mysticism. Many Jews emigrated to the Holy Land, and in upper Galilee, there gathered a prestigious group of scholars. Its prestige was enhanced by being the place where the Mishnah by Judah ha-Nasi was supposed to have been composed and, it was thought, the *Zohar* by Simeon ben Yohai, as well. It had intrinsic attractiveness for Jewish mystics. This physical disruption and relocation helped encourage a form of Kabbalism that embraced the realities of history. The theme of transmigration of souls, metempsychosis (in Hebrew, gilgul), had already existed in earlier Kabbalism, but now the notion of souls leaving one body at death and entering into another body could be joined to the notion of the people's exile and restoration. Just as an individual loses the self and gains a self in another body, so do the people lose a self in exile and gain their self in restoration; the mysticism is not only about the individual but the people as a whole. And as a result, Messianism begins to emerge again as a hope for the restoration of the people. Messianism, in this Lurianic Safed spirituality, reenters the mythology of the Kabbalah.

It was certainly not geography alone that made Safed the new center of Kabbalism, but the fact that concurrently, three great mystical teachers were present in that town—two of them also great visionaries. The first of these teachers is Rabbi Joseph ben Ephraim Karo, whose dates are 1488–1575. He is well known in Judaism as the great authority on Jewish Law. He is the author of the *Shulchan Arukh*, the standard code of Law, which is still an authoritative text for Jews today. But he was also a great mystic who received revelations about Torah and Kabbalah from a heavenly maggid, a messenger, a mentor, somebody who delivered messages to him from heaven.

We have extant a firsthand testimony to one of these ecstatic incidents, written by Solomon Alkabetz, whose dates are 1505–1576, who was a student of Joseph Karo. And here is what he says:

> No sooner had we studied two tractates of the Mishnah than our Creator smote us so that we heard a voice speaking out of the mouth of the saint ... [the saint in this case is Karo, so there's a voice that is coming from him] may his light shine. It was a loud voice with letters clearly enunciated. All the companions heard the voice but were unable to understand what was said. It was an exceedingly pleasant voice, becoming increasingly strong. We all fell on our faces and none of us had any spirit left in him because of great dread and awe. The voice began to address us, saying, Friends, choicest of the choice, peace to you beloved companions. My friends, rejoice and exalt for you belong among the chosen few. You have the merit of belonging to the king's palace. The sound of your Torah and the breath of your mouth have ascended to the Holy One, blessed be He, breaking through many firmaments and many atmospheres until it came upwards.

This experience of Joseph Karo was not simply the experience of an individual privately. It took place in a group of his disciples, and one of his disciples recorded it. We also have extant, in fact, the mystical diary of Joseph Karo, in which he kept a journal of the various mystical experiences that he had. Here is a sample, "the eve of Sabbath 22nd Adar," the month of Adar. Now, in this journal entry, it is the maggid speaking to Joseph Karo, so he records what he hears:

> The Lord be with you but only if you cleave to Me and do not separate your thoughts even for a single moment from My Mishnah. [That is the Law.] Eat not and drink not for your own enjoyment at all. What profit is there in the pleasures of this world? Rather your thoughts should be: If it were possible to keep body and soul together without having any pleasure, you would greatly desire such a state. In this way you will cleave always to God and miracles will be performed on your behalf just as they were performed on behalf of the ancient saints and people will know that there is a God in Israel.

The voice is telling Karo, stick to your task, study the Mishnah, and as a result, you please God, and great deeds will be done through you. He has another extended vision in which he hears what is awaiting him. He is promised that he may actually be able to die as a martyr for the Lord, and then he will be drawn into heaven:

> All the saints in the Garden of Eden, the *Shekinah* at their head, will come out to meet you, welcoming you with many songs and praises. They will lead you like a groom who walks in front, and they will accompany you to your canopy. [It's a sacred marriage that will take place in heaven.] I have prepared for you seven canopies, one within the other, and seven canopies, one higher than other. [What does this sound like to us? The seven heavens that we saw in earlier mystical treatises: "seven canopies, one within the other, ... seven canopies, one above the other."] Within the innermost and highest of canopies there will be seven rivers of fragrant balsam.

So Joseph Karo has these kinds of experiences, and we see that one of the features of Lurianic Kabbalism is a very great emphasis upon ecstatic states, of very powerful mystical experiences in the classic sense of the term.

The second great mystical teacher in Safed was not a visionary; he was much more of a scholar. His name is Rabbi Moses ben Jacob Cordovero. His dates are 1522–1570. He was a prolific writer and scholar who produced a large body of work before his death at 48. His works include a massive commentary on the *Zohar*, but he was something of a philosopher of Kabbalism. He was more systematic in his thinking, and in particular, Cordovero was preoccupied by trying to figure out the relationship between the great problem that I identified in previous lectures, the problem of transcendence of God and the immanence of God. If God is one, how can God at once be totally other than the world and yet present in the world? And we saw in the *Zohar* how this is configured in terms of *Eyn Sof*, God in God's self, and the *sefirot*, the emanations of God. For Cordovero, this relationship finally is stated quite cryptically in a proposition which is profoundly paradoxical: "God is all reality, but not all reality is God." If this proposition, "God is all reality, but not all reality is God," strikes you as being dense, it is because the problem is very dense. And we will see similar statements, above all, in Sufi Mysticism, where the same problem of the oneness of God and the unity of God in creation is struggled with by one mystical thinker after the other.

By far, the most influential of the three great mystics in Safed is Isaac Luria. He is sometimes called Ari, which means "the Lion." His dates are 1534–1572. He was the most influential figure in the future shaping of Jewish Mysticism. He was a learned man, he was a scholar, but as far as we know for certain, he wrote only one book. His teaching is conveyed mainly through the works of his disciples, so one problem we have with Isaac Luria is sort of sorting out what really comes from him and what is filtered through the interpretations of his scholars. What is clear is that in his life, Isaac Luria was a noted visionary. He seems to be one of those mystics who best fits our stereotypical picture of a mystic, somebody who is wandering around, always somewhere else, sort of a distracted type of person. He sees souls as residing in all things. He visits the graves of the saints of the past. He is convinced that he bears within himself the souls of those figures in the past and, above all, the prophet Elijah. He has a very intense understanding of metempsychosis, or the transmigration of souls.

Luria's most important interpreter is his student Hayyim Vital, whose dates are 1543–1620. Hayyim Vital records his own mystical experiences; he doesn't report on those of his master, but he himself has visions in his *Sefer ha-Chezyonot*, the *Book of Visions*, that he compiled between the years 1609–1612. This is a sample, in the year 5338 [this is Jewish dating; it equals 1578]:

> On Sabbath morning, I was preaching to the congregation in Jerusalem. Rachel, the sister of Rabbi Judah Mishnah, was present. She told me that during the whole of my sermon there was a pillar of fire above my head and Elijah of blessed memory was there at my right hand to support me and that when I had finished they both departed. Also in Damascus in the year 1602, she saw a pillar of fire above my head when I conducted the *Musaf* service in the Sicilian community on the Day of Atonement. This woman is wont to see visions, demons, spirits and angels and she has been accurate in most of her statements from the time [that] she was a little girl until now that she has grown to womanhood.

The picture here is of Hayyim preaching, and the divine presence in a pillar of fire and the great prophet Elijah are there accompanying him and visible to those to whom he is preaching. Another entry in Hayyim Vital's journal, this one dated 1571:

> The New Moon of the month of Iyyar. At the time of the afternoon prayer I went into isolation by the means known to me of reciting three times the Mishnah text. [He moves himself into an ecstatic trance by the repetition of a text from the Mishnah.] I had it in mind to inquire about my previous incarnation. [This is the point of his mystical journey.] I fell into a trance and saw my master of blessed memory, who said to me: "Behold, this handsome young man standing beside us is my brother-in-law, my sister's husband, and you were his teacher." Then I awoke. [This a dream trance.] I recited the Mishnah once again and fell asleep. I heard a very loud voice calling "Hayyim! Hayyim!" and I was afraid and I awoke. I thought to myself that my master of blessed memory was Rabban Gamaliel, the brother-in-law of Rabbi Eliezer, disciple of Rabban Johanan ben Zakkai.

The significance of these three figures is that he is perceiving that his master Ari, or Isaac Luria, is accompanied or, rather, possesses the souls of three of the greatest rabbis of the earliest period in the rabbinic tradition, Gamaliel, Eliezer, and Johanan ben Zakkai.

I went to my master and I related [all this too him but] he said: "This is undoubtedly a heavenly visitation; yet I do not wish to reveal to you the meaning of it because I do not wish you to know the previous incarnation of my soul."

These two citations from Joseph Karo and Hayyim Vital point us to certain themes in Lurianic Mysticism. One of them is the transmigration of the souls, the sense of being in contact with or even incarnating figures from the past. Another is an emphasis upon the visionary, and the third is an emphasis upon the individual mystic as a public figure who manifests the presence of God miraculously through mysticism. All of these threads we will see developed in both fortunate and unfortunate ways in the future. This Lurianic vision of Kabbalism was propagated throughout Europe, especially by Israel Sarug, who traveled into the Ashkenazi communities in Northern Europe between 1592–1598, spreading the message of this new version of Kabbalism, which was much more democratic. It was much more rooted in the person, rather than in the text. I don't want to make that disjunction too severe; the study of the text was still there, as we saw. The reading of the Mishnah and so forth functioned as a way into ecstatic states, but the point was much more than realizing ecstatic conditions.

Lurianic Kabbalism shapes the Kabbalistic tradition in a manner that has far-reaching implications. It is perhaps closer to the Prophetic Kabbalism of Abraham Abulafia that we saw in an earlier lecture in its emphasis on personal asceticism and the practice of mysticism. Practical Mysticism has two meanings. As might be expected in a group with such visionary experiences, there is an emphasis on the ways of achieving such states, although technique is mostly handed on orally rather than in writing. But Practical Kabbalism can also mean theurgy, or magic, that is, the manipulation of reality through the manipulation of symbols in order to bring about certain results. A fascinating aspect of this in Safed spirituality is the practice of phrenology. Phrenology is the study of the bumps on the head, and we find evidence in Lurianic texts that this was a very serious aspect of mystical study. If we think about it for a moment, we see the logic: If the divine emanations, the *sefirot*, as we saw in the previous presentation, took the form of a figurative body; and the top of that body, the *keter*, is the high point; and if humans are made in the image of God; and these *sefirot* should be present in humans, it would make sense that by studying the configuration of the top of one's head, one would diagnostically be able to understand whether or not one is in good shape as a mystic. And this was the sort of practice in which the Safed mystics engaged.

Three elements of theosophy—that is, the understanding of cosmic reality—in particular, are developed in a more powerfully mythic, even a Gnostic, direction. We really are moving with Lurianic Mysticism to something far more powerfully mythic even than in the *Zohar*. The first of these elements is called *tsimtsum*, which means "concentration" and/or "withdrawal." This is the notion that creation becomes possible, the world becomes possible, because God as *Eyn Sof* withdraws God's self and concentrates God's self, leaving, if you will, space for creation. There is this sense of the relationship between *Eyn Sof* and *sefirot* as a kind of ebb and flow, that the *sefirot* are not only coming out of God, but are being exiled from God. There is a kind of self-exile going on, and therefore, for *Eyn Sof* to be complete, the *sefirot* also need to be restored to God so that God is, if you will, virtually self-exiled in creation. And the sparks of divine light, then, are in the darkness of creation and need be retrieved.

A second important notion that develops here, equally strange, *shevirrath ha-Kelim*, the "breaking of the vessels." This is a notion, which is highly anthropomorphic, of a cosmic disruption that is somehow connected to the overwhelming effect of the three great *sefirot*, the *keter*, hokhmah, and *binah*, on the primordial human— not an actual human but the primordial cosmic human, Adam Kadmon, archetypal human—that creates a disruption that involves both the cosmos and humans, so that both the world and humans, if you will, are broken vessels. There's damage there. Evil in the world is seen as a result of this separation, disruption. Again, we can hear echoes of exiles in this.

The third theme that enters in, then—which was anticipated in Kabbalah but now becomes even more important—is *tikkun*, the notion of "mending" or "uniting." And this points us to the cosmic role of humans. By keeping the Commandments and by their adherence to God's word, *devequt*, to that body of Torah, through their strict intention, *kawwanah*, the mystic helps mend the world. Every individual Jew, every mystic in Judaism has this role of helping to mend the world by not only keeping the Commandments but by adhering to Torah in their minds. In short, the mystic plays a crucial role in the great cosmic drama of God's self emptying and return of rays scattered into creation, like so many sparks, and gathered again through human effort; and of bringing about the Messianic Age through the efforts of faithful Israel and the work of mystics.

Safed's spirituality is also noteworthy because it extends into the mainstream of Jewish life everywhere it is practiced. It represents something of a democratization of spirituality into Judaism. It made certain ascetical practices, such as fasting, standard for the Jewish community, and it was Luria's prescriptions for penitents that replaced those of the German Hasidim everywhere. It contributed a mystical element to the standard Jewish liturgy. Hymns that were written and prayers that were written from the perspective of this breaking and mending of the world entered into the Jewish liturgy and affected both individuals and communities who prayed to them. Above all, Lurianic Mysticism provided a unifying vision for Jews everywhere of their participation in a divine drama of loss and redemption, a divine drama in which humans were deeply involved and in which the divine element in humans was absolutely required if the divine drama was to reach a satisfying resolution.

Even writings of a deeply ethical character that we would not think of as being particularly mystical in character show the deep imprint of Lurianic Mysticism. I take as an example the *Sheney Luhot ha-Berit, The Two Tablets of the Covenant*, that is written by Isaiah ben Abraham Horowitz, whose dates are 1570–1626. It is suffused with the sensibility of Lurianic Kabbalah. I'm quoting two small segments from the introduction to this massive work, which itself is quite a large book called *The Generations of Adam*. The first short citation speaks of the relationship between external observance and internal mysticism. He says:

> Also prayer, the service of our heart which has replaced Temple offerings which bring one close and cause us to cleave to the Blessed One, must be a prayer with *kavvanah* [with intention]. Then it is a body with a soul [the exoteric with the esoteric]. The "body" of the prayer is the order that has been arranged for us by our sages of blessed memory and fear and trembling [these are the words that we say], while its "soul" is the *kavvanah*, the secrets of prayer.

The inner meaning of prayer is the intention, the heart with which the mystic prays. And as he continues his work, Horowitz tells his readers that he stands in the long tradition of Simeon ben Yohai and his associates, the *Zohar*, and of Isaac Luria. And he can't hope to add much to what those great teachers said, but he does say:

> I will add a bit of what I have arrived at with my own understanding in uniting the various matters in order to comprehend them. It is known that holiness is an endless spring.

> If a person sanctifies himself a bit below, he is sanctified a lot from above and the Holy One will grace him with wisdom, understanding, and knowledge. Then he will merit to enter the innermost chambers, through many myriad good levels to the Presence, blessed be He.

Lecture Ten
Sabbatai Zevi and Messianic Mysticism

Scope:

The elements of mysticism and Messianism that had gathered in Lurianic mysticism found an explosive and paradoxical expression in the figure of Sabbatai Zevi. Zevi's self-proclamation as Messiah and subsequent apostasy from Judaism in 1665–1666 caused a mass movement of excitement among Jews in Europe. A sectarian movement (Sabbatianism) emerged that combined elements of Kabbalism with antinomian tendencies, in sharp contrast to the halachic piety of all previous Jewish Mysticism. This lecture traces the career of Sabbatai Zevi and his chief propagandist, Nathan of Gaza, as well as the subsequent shape of the movement that took his name.

Outline

I. The Jewish mystical tradition developed over the centuries, slowly, quietly, and in circles of intense textual analysis, but when we turn to Sabbatai Zevi (1626–1676) and Messianic Mysticism, we find something new and dangerous, both for Jewish Mysticism and for Judaism as a whole.

   A. There were many messianic pretenders in the 1st century.
   1. Jesus of Nazareth was thought by some to be a Messiah but was rejected by the majority of Jews.
   2. Bar Kochba had been proclaimed Messiah by Rabbi Akiva in the revolt of 135 but was discovered not to have restored the people.

   B. Mysticism always tests exoteric traditions by its emphasis on inner devotion more than external observance, and each religious tradition has an example of mysticism becoming heretical.
   1. In Christianity, Gnosticism was rejected for its denial of central truths concerning Jesus.
   2. In Islam, Hallaj is repudiated by the majority of Muslims because he is thought to have compromised the oneness of Allah.
   3. In Judaism, the Sabbatian movement was declared heretical because of its principled antinomianism. That

©2008 The Teaching Company.

is, it took a stand against the observance of Torah in a fundamental way, while claiming to be Jewish.

C. Judaism in the 17th century was primed for the explosion caused by Zevi by a number of internal and external factors.

1. The 17th century was a time of external repression for Judaism. The establishment of the ghetto in Venice in 1516 was a disturbing portent of things to come, such as the Chmielnitzki pogrom in 1648.

2. In England, Christian millenarian speculation identified 1666 as the apocalyptic year, when the Messiah would appear.

3. Lurianic Kabbalism had fused notions about the transmigration of souls, exile, and restoration (*tikkun*) with a messianic expectation connected to the efforts of mystics.

4. Some Kabbalists had identified 1648 as the year when the Messiah would appear to restore the people.

II. The sequence of events in the rise of Sabbatai Zevi is fairly clear; more difficult is assessing his character.

A. He was born in present-day Turkey, and his father worked for an English company in Smyrna. As a young man, Zevi studied Talmud and Kabbalah according to the teaching of Isaac Luria.

1. He was married twice, but his wives were granted divorces as a result of his extreme asceticism. He experienced swings between ecstasy and melancholy.

2. He first claimed to be Messiah in 1648 in Smyrna and pronounced the divine name (the tetragrammaton), leading to his excommunication by the college of rabbis and his banishment, along with his followers, in 1651.

B. Zevi embarked on a life of wandering through the Mediterranean world, arriving in Constantinople in 1653. There, Abraham ha-Yakini produced a forged document claiming that Zevi was the Messiah.

C. In Salonica, Zevi declared himself married to *Eyn Sof* and was again banished.

1. He traveled to Cairo, Jerusalem, and back to Cairo.

2. In Cairo, he married Sarah, a survivor of a pogrom who had worked as a prostitute and was convinced that she was to be the bride of the Messiah.

D. A young man named Nathan of Gaza became Zevi's advocate and announced in 1665 that the Messianic Age would begin the next year.

1. With his followers, Zevi reached Smyrna in the fall of 1665 and, on the New Year, proclaimed himself Messiah.

2. This announcement caused incredible excitement throughout Europe, leading many Jews to place their faith in Zevi as the Messiah and disrupt their lives in preparation for the coming age.

3. Zevi began to issue decrees concerning observance, changing fast days into days of celebration; those who did not obey were suppressed.

E. He was eventually arrested by the Muslim ruler of Istanbul and brought before Sultan Mehmed IV on September 16, 1666. Instead of martyrdom, Zevi chose conversion to Islam.

1. Between the time of his apostasy and his death in 1676, Zevi maintained that he was actually in service to God in both traditions.

2. He succeeded in bringing some Muslims to his Kabbalistic views and some Jews to Islam, creating a Judeo-Turkish sect based on faith in him.

F. Evaluating the character of Sabbatai Zevi is difficult: Was he a sincere if sick individual or a manipulative charlatan?

1. In Gershom Scholem's reading, Zevi was a manic-depressive who was mainly the passive instrument of Nathan of Gaza.

2. In another reading, he was a notoriety seeker who manipulated events to secure his own fame.

III. The movement called Sabbatianism did not end with Sabbatai Zevi's apostasy from Judaism.

A. In a classic case of cognitive dissonance resolved, the fact of Zevi's apostasy was reinterpreted according to the tenets of Lurianic Kabbalism.

1. His apostasy was actually a form of self-exile, an entering into the abyss of evil.

2. Restoration will be in the future, with the return of Zevi as the triumphant Messiah.

B. Although rejected by other Jews, perhaps hundreds of thousands of Sabbatians continued as believers and practiced the ritual breaking of the Commandments.

Recommended Reading:

Scholem, G. *Sabbatai Zevi: The Mystical Messiah (1626–1676).*

Questions to Consider:

1. Identify the points of similarity and dissimilarity in the messianic careers of Sabbatai Zevi and Jesus of Nazareth.

2. Discuss the concept of "cognitive dissonance" and its usefulness in analyzing powerful social movements.

Lecture Ten—Transcript
Sabbatai Zevi and Messianic Mysticism

The Jewish mystical tradition developed over the centuries, slowly, quietly, and in circles of intense textual analysis. Whether we speak of the Merkabah mystics of ancient Palestine or the Hasidim of medieval Germany, the early Kabbalists of Gerona, or the adepts of the *Zohar*, we find such quiet, truly esoteric circles of study within the Jewish community. And throughout, Jewish Mysticism was always deeply connected to the essence of Jewish life—that is, the observance of God's Commandments that are found in Torah. With Safed spirituality, with the spirituality that's mostly identified with Isaac Luria, we noted a new level of popularization or democratization of mysticism; a much greater level of drama, of mythology; and above all, a concentration on individual figures as ecstatics, as visionaries. We finally saw a connection between mysticism and Messianism in Lurianic spirituality.

However, when we turn to the figure of Sabbatai Zevi and Messianic Mysticism, we find something new and dangerous, both for Jewish Mysticism and for Judaism as a whole. In the middle of the 17th century, the Jewish mystical tradition saw the emergence of a messianic figure, Sabbatai Zevi, whose dates are 1626–1676. There had been other messianic figures in the history of Judaism. There were many messianic pretenders in the 1st century; Jesus of Nazareth was thought by some to be a Messiah but was rejected by the majority of Jews. Bar Kochba had been proclaimed Messiah by Rabbi Akiva in the revolt of 135 but was discovered not to have restored the people. What made Sabbatai Zevi different from those messianic figures? What made him different was that he created an acute crisis at the very heart of Judaism, cut to the very essence of Judaism, and did so in a public and pervasive way so that it was a shock to the entire Jewish system, what happened in Sabbatai Zevi.

We will learn, progressively, that mysticism always tests exoteric traditions by its emphasis on inner devotion more than external observance. The problem is: When does "more than" become "instead of" external observance? Each tradition has an example of mysticism becoming heretical. We will see in Christianity that Gnosticism is rejected for its rejection of central truths concerning Jesus, namely, that he was not only divine but also human, that he not only saved souls but also saved bodies. The Gnostics' denial of these central truths meant that they were rejected by the majority of Christians. We will see in Islam that Hallaj is repudiated by the majority of Muslims, because he was thought to compromise the oneness of Allah, the most central conviction of that tradition. He made statements in ecstasy that seemed to identify himself with Allah and, therefore, was perceived to be giving partners to Allah, the most unforgivable form of apostasy within Islam. In Judaism, similarly, this Sabbatian movement becomes heretical because of its principled antinomianism. That is, it took a stand against the observance of Torah in a fundamental way, while claiming to be Jewish.

The 17th century was primed for such an explosion because of a combination of internal and external factors. Externally, it was a time of increased repression. The establishment of the ghetto in Venice in 1516 was a disturbing portent of things to come. Jews previous to this had suffered from controlling laws, but if they lived together, it was out of choice. They wore the clothing of other people. In Venice in 1516, Jews were required to live in a single quarter of that city called Ghetto. They were required to return to that quarter at night. They were required to wear identifying clothing that set them apart even more. Jewish existence, in short, became closer to imprisonment than simple marginalization. A dangerous pogrom, or attack on the Jews, occurred in 1648 Chmielnitzki in Eastern Europe. It became clear that Jews were under threat more and more, and the conviction began to arise that the Messiah surely will come when the people suffer sufficiently. This is a characteristic sort of psychological move connected to apocalyptic thinking: that things must get worse and worse, and when they finally reach their nadir, then God will intervene to save his people. So the external atmosphere was one that was not congenial to Jews.

Furthermore, Christian millenarianism, Christian expectation of the end of the world, was lively during this time. In England, the year 1666 had been identified as the apocalyptic year, when the Messiah, Jesus, would return. This was so well known that the Jewish Rabbi Menasseh ben Israel wrote to Oliver Cromwell asking the Rump Parliament to allow Jews to reenter England, from which they had been expelled on this very basis. He says, "The opinions of many Christians and mine do concur therein, that we both believe that the restoring time of our nation into their native country is very near at hand." The logic here is: Why not let them back into England since they're shortly going to be leaving for Palestine because the Messiah is coming?

A third factor is that Lurianic Kabbalism, which we briefly studied in the previous presentation, had, as we saw, fused notions about the transmigration of souls (so that present-day individuals could be inhabited by previous souls); exile; restoration, or *tikkun*, and a messianic expectation connected to the work and the efforts of mystics. We saw that Lurianic Mysticism had an extraordinary attention paid to spectacular figures who did not sit hunched over the study of Torah, but who wandered the streets in ecstatic condition, who claimed to have visions and heavenly portents and were seen by others to have such experiences. Indeed, Rabbi Isaac Luria himself was thought to be inhabited by the messianic forerunner, the prophet Elijah. All of these things are coming together in Lurianic Kabbalism.

And, finally, some Kabbalists, through the analysis of Torah text and the practice of gematria, the supplying of numbers, had identified 1648 as the year when the Jewish Messiah would return to restore the people. The atmosphere was set; the context was set. The internal mechanisms were in order. The calculations were set. All of these things primed the situation for the rising of a false Messiah, Sabbatai Zevi. The sequence of events, a sad sequence of events, is fairly clear. More difficult is assessing the character of Sabbatai Zevi. He appears to be a person who is acting out an internal script. He is not only aware of being a dramatic figure, he is one of those persons who lives in public, somebody who acts out a role in public.

He was born in present-day Turkey. His father was a man who worked for an English trading company in Smyrna, and the distinct possibility is there that Sabbatai Zevi would have been aware of these English millenarian expectations at a very early age. As a very young man, Sabbatai Zevi studied Talmud and Kabbalah according to the teaching of Isaac Luria, so he had ingested the notions of exile and restoration, the notion of present persons being embodiments of previous existences through transmigration. He was married twice but was so ascetical in his practices that his wives were granted divorce, so he was granted two divorces. Perhaps most notable is that he is perceived by outsiders as somebody who experiences wide swings psychologically between states of exaltation or ecstasy, in which he carries out provocative acts of all sorts, followed by a deep swing of melancholy. Of course, today, we would perhaps term this manic-depressive disorder or bipolar disease, but it is clear that these are the swings through which Sabbatai Zevi went.

He first comes to public attention by claiming to be the Messiah in 1648, one of the dates that had been determined by the Kabbalists. He does this in Smyrna when he is 22 years old, and he does this by pronouncing the divine name in public, the tetragrammaton. To understand the provocative character of this act, we must remember that the name of the Lord, the proper name of God, YHWH, is never pronounced by pious Jews. When they come across that word in the Bible, they will replace it with another word, like Memra or Adonai. It is not pronounced publicly; it's not pronounced in worship. The only time it is announced is by the high priest on the Day of Atonement. By pronouncing the tetragrammaton, the four-letter word, publicly in 1648, Sabbatai Zevi clearly signals to the world that he is somebody who will become Messiah by breaking the Law. That's the fundamental move. This leads to his excommunication by the college of rabbis in that area. He's put under herem, under the ban, and he and his followers are banished from Turkey in 1651.

He then enters into a period of wandering, exile, if you will, through the Mediterranean world. He arrived in Constantinople in 1653 and stayed there for about six years. While there, he showed his distinctive capability of gathering disciples. He was clearly a charismatic, that is, a highly attractive figure. A man named Abraham ha-Yakini was one of his followers and produced what is obviously a forged writing that he claimed was the great wisdom of Solomon. That writing declared that Sabbatai Zevi was going to be the Messiah in words such as this:

> I, Abraham, was confined in the cave for 40 years, and I wondered greatly that the time of miracles did not arrive. Then was heard a voice proclaiming, "A son will be born in the Hebrew year 5386 [that's 1626, which happens to be Sabbatai Zevi's birthday] to Mordecai Zevi; and he will be called Shabbethai. He will humble the great dragon. He, the true Messiah, will sit upon My throne.

One of his followers in Constantinople "discovers" this prophetic text, which declares Sabbatai Zevi as the Messiah. He then wanders through Alexandria, Athens, Constantinople, Jerusalem, back to Smyrna. He ends up in the city of Salonica, where he declares himself son of God and has performed a symbolic marriage between himself, as son of God, and *Eyn Sof*—that is, the Godhead. He is, not surprisingly, banished because of this action, and he ends up in Cairo in Egypt, where he spent a period of time and made acquaintances and supporters out of some very wealthy folks in that city.

From there, he traveled to Jerusalem, and the account says that Sabbatai Zevi looked very much like a contemporary politician would look in Jerusalem, gathering favor. He had a sweet singing voice, and he would sing in public and draw people to himself. He would pray publicly and spectacularly at the graves of previous saints. He would even shamelessly distribute candy to children. All of these things made him a highly visible and very popular character in Jerusalem. And the opportunity arose for him to return to Cairo, ostensibly to raise money from his wealthy friends for the community in Jerusalem, which was needy. While in Cairo, he did marry (for the final time) a woman named Sarah, who was a survivor of a pogrom in Europe and had spent the intervening time working as a prostitute. What singled out Sarah was that she was convinced that she was to be the bride of the Messiah, so this clearly was a match made in heaven. He thought he was the Messiah; she thought she was destined to marry the Messiah.

But, again, given the fact that especially in Jewish lore and in various kinds of ways of thinking, Jesus of Nazareth was thought to be associated with a loose woman, Mary Magdalene, again, you see the issue of whether or not Sabbatai Zevi was deliberately walking according to a script of an antinomian Messiah. We will remember that Jesus was an antinomian Messiah. Jesus broke the Sabbath laws. Jesus broke laws of purity. So this is a perennial sort of issue. To what extent is Sabbatai Zevi actually following the script that was written first by the Christian Messiah, Jesus?

At this point in his career, Sabbatai Zevi meets the person who is going to be most critical for the future, Nathan of Gaza. Gershom Scholem, who puts almost everything in the hands of Nathan of Gaza, calls him "Sabbatai Zevi's John the Baptist and Paul the Apostle." In other words, he was both the one who announced him as Messiah and then the one who propagated him as Messiah. He was Sabbatai Zevi's great advocate, and he announced in the year 1665 that the Messianic Age would begin the following year, in 1666. Sabbatai picked up on this, and spread the announcement, and added considerable amount of details: that he embodied Elijah, that he would conquer the world without bloodshed, and that he would lead back to Israel—and this is important—the 10 lost tribes. The Messiah is the one who restores the people by bringing them back to Israel, and he would do this riding on a lion with a seven-headed dragon in its jaws. And such claims were widely circulated. The rabbis in Jerusalem were not impressed. They repel him another time, and he finds his way back to Smyrna.

With his followers in Smyrna—and the followers greeted him with great enthusiasm—in the fall of 1665, he arrives in Smyrna and, on the New Year, proclaims himself as the Messiah. The declaration was made in the context of synagogue worship with the blowing of the *shofar*, the horns, and he was greeted by his followers in the synagogue of Smyrna: "Long live our king, our Messiah." In effect, part of the Jewish population proclaimed him as Messiah. This announcement created a huge amount of excitement throughout Europe, and for us to begin to appreciate the sort of cataclysmic character of this, we have to understand that this is long before the days of newspapers and telecommunication; the instantaneous character of the responses made to this figure speaks for a rapid word-of-mouth transmission by travelers and so forth throughout Europe. A German intellectual wrote to Baruch Spinoza, an excommunicated Jew, that "All the world here is talking of a rumor of the return of the Israelites to their own country. ... Should the news be confirmed, it may bring about a revolution in all things." This is widely enough known to reach intellectual circles in Europe. People were excited everywhere; this led many Jews to put their faith in him as the Messiah and disrupt their lives. The Jewish community in Avignon, France, prepared to emigrate to the new kingdom in the spring of 1666. In fact, some people began to take the roofs off their houses in order to get to the new world that was being created by Sabbatai Zevi.

For the psychology here, I would recommend Norman Cohn's wonderful book *The Pursuit of the Millennium*, because he shows how the combination of millenarian expectations and external oppression can generate a circumstance in which those who are experiencing hard things can, when news of a change is imminent, engage in the most extravagant gestures—leaving their homes, selling their houses, moving to another place in order to grasp on to the hope that is being offered by a messianic figure. Being greeted by the folks in Smyrna as the Messiah, Sabbatai Zevi begins to issue decrees concerning the observance or, perhaps better, non-observance of the Law. He changes fast days, for example (remember, Yom Kippur is the great day of fasting, the Day of Atonement.), into days of celebration. He declares:

> The first begotten Son of God, Sabbatai Zevi, Messiah and Redeemer of the people of Israel to all the sons of Israel, Peace. Since ye have been deemed worthy to behold the great day and the fulfillment of God's word by the Prophets, your lament and sorrow must be changed into joy and your fasting into merriment; for ye shall weep no more. Rejoice with song and melody and change the day formerly spent in sadness and sorrow into a day of jubilee, because I have appeared.

Once more, we hear an echo of an earlier Messiah. There's a statement in the Gospels attributed to Jesus in which he declares that people cannot fast while the bridegroom is present with them; they can only fast when the bridegroom is absent, and when the bridegroom is there, they should feast. Sabbatai Zevi is consciously or unconsciously echoing the same sort of thing. The fasting was carried out because the great Messiah was not there. Now that the Messiah is here, we need to feast. The implication, of course, though, is that Torah is temporary, and Torah can be overruled by a mystical messianic figure. He began to issue such decrees, even exercising the sort of tyrannical spirit that apparently was there from the beginning and began to ban and suppress Jews in that community who didn't obey these sorts of commands.

All of this became too much for everybody, and he was eventually arrested by the Muslim ruler of Istanbul, ancient Constantinople, which was now a Muslim city, and he spent several months in the pokey undergoing very lenient treatment. He continued to issue decrees as the Messiah. Tales were spread about his miracles, and some Jews in Europe prepared for the new Exodus. For example, on Passover, he slew a lamb for himself and his followers and ate it together with its fat, which was against the dietary regulations, and he pronounced the benediction over the lamb: "Blessed be the God who has restored again that which was forbidden." So he, as the Messiah, is superior to Torah. In parts of Europe, as I said, people began to tear off their roofs and prepare, sell their possessions, and move to the Holy Land. In almost every synagogue in Europe, Sabbatai Zevi's initials were posted. Prayers for him were inserted into the set prayers in the synagogue: "Bless our Lord and King, the holy and righteous, Sabbatai Zevi, the Messiah of the God of Jacob."

This lenient period of imprisonment was followed by a more serious arrest and trial before the Muslim Sultan Mehmed IV on September 16, 1666. Here we have Sabbatai Zevi facing an imperial power, again, like Jesus does before Pontius Pilate. This is the chance for him to die as a martyr, to witness to the reality of Torah and to the God of Torah. What does Sabbatai Zevi do? He casts off his Jewish clothing, puts on a turban, and declares himself to be Muslim. He simply apostatizes from Judaism and becomes a Muslim. As a reward, he is made a minor official by the sultan, and he begins to take on more wives, according to the regulations of the Shari'ah. He declares, "God has made me an Ishmaelite"—that is, a son of Abraham through Ishmael. "He commanded, and it was done, the ninth day of my regeneration."

Between the time of his apostasy and his death in 1676, a period of about 10 years, Sabbatai Zevi maintained that he was actually consistent; he was in service to God in both traditions. And he succeeded in bringing some Muslims to his own version of Kabbalism and some Jews to Islam, creating a Judeo-Turkish sect that was distinguished by its faith in him. As I said, evaluating the character of Sabbatai Zevi is difficult. Was he a sincere if sick person or a manipulative charlatan? In Gershom Scholem's reading, he is a manic-depressive who is mainly the passive instrument of Nathan of Gaza. In another reading, which I tend to favor, he is a well-known type in sociology, the notoriety seeker, the person who needs to be at the center of attention, and he did whatever was required to secure his own fame. He knew the script, and he acted according to the script.

The movement called Sabbatianism, remarkably, did not end with Sabbatai Zevi's apostasy. Here, we have a classic case of the resolution of cognitive dissonance. He says he's the Messiah, but he apostatizes. In order for us to continue in our convictions, we need to reinterpret his apostasy in the light of the tenets of Lurianic Kabbalism. So his apostasy was actually a form of self-exile, an entering into the realm of evil, the abyss of evil, and his restoration will be in the future. Just as Christians expected the return of their

Messiah, Jesus, in the future, so do Sabbatians expect the return of Sabbatai Zevi in the future. Although this movement was rejected by the majority of Jews, hundreds of thousands of them continued as believers and practiced the ritual breaking of the Commandments.

Lecture Eleven
The Ba'al Shem Tov and the New Hasidism

Scope:

In the 18th century, a new form of Jewish Mysticism arose in Eastern Europe, beginning with the charismatic career of Israel Ba'al Shem Tov ("Master of the Good Name"), around whom were collected many tales of wisdom and wonder-working. This New Hasidism was a more popular form of mysticism. It pervaded the community as a whole rather than just a small group of scholars and was focused on the spirit-filled *tzaddik*, the popular leader and center of the community, more so than the learned rabbi. The basic conceptions of this Hasidism remained similar to those of Kabbalism, but the ideas were rendered in more popular form. This lecture considers the life of the founder of the New Hasidism, the progression of the movement, and the character of its literature and piety.

Outline

I. The rise and fall of Sabbatai Zevi, the mystical Messiah, created a severe crisis for Jewish Mysticism.

   A. The Lurianic form of Kabbalism that had spread so widely across the synagogues of Europe now appeared as potentially dangerous. Nonetheless, mysticism did not disappear entirely, and in this lecture, we consider the last great development in Jewish Mysticism with the Ba'al Shem Tov and the New Hasidism.

   B. Hasidism arose in Eastern Europe in the 18th century amid both new and old challenges for Jews. For example, the persecution of Jews through pogroms continued sporadically during this period.

   C. Jewish traditional observance was also threatened by the Haskalah, the Enlightenment, which was taking place in Europe at this time and called into question the entire symbolic world of Torah.

   1. Baruch Spinoza (1632–1677) was one of the first influential critics of the Bible. He tested the stories in the Bible against the measure of the Enlightenment and found those stories to be either historically or

scientifically impossible. For Spinoza, the Bible was not true, but it was still meaningful.

   2. At the same time, Spinoza's pantheistic view of reality echoed the vision of Kabbalism.

D. Sabbatianism continued to divide Jewish communities, particularly with the rise of Jacob Frank (1726–1791), a follower of Sabbatai Zevi and another false Messiah who also apostasized, this time, to Christianity.

E. While Judaism thrived in its Talmudic form in urban centers that offered stable conditions, in the Ukraine, where Hasidism arose, Jews were scattered in rural villages with no centers of learning.

F. Hasidism emerged in these conditions as a powerful form of popular mysticism that was centered in the transformation of individuals more than the study of texts, focused on ecstatic joy more than penitential sorrow.

II. The Hasidic movement was deeply marked by the charismatic nature of its founder, Rabbi Israel ben Eliezer, the Ba'al Shem Tov (also called Besht, 1698–1760).

A. Besht was a simple and poor man, a lover of nature, and not a scholar.

   1. His poverty was acute, and he held a series of simple jobs throughout his life, including minding a village tavern. He and his wife, Chana, had two children.

   2. He served as a sexton in the synagogue and a mediator in the Jewish community but gained fame as a healer, inscribing amulets and prescribing herbs for the sick. He had the gift of controlling the divine name; thus, he was known as Ba'al Shem Tov, "Master of the Good Name."

B. Besht began gathering followers and started teaching in Medzhybizh around 1740; even members of the educated elite came to hear him.

   1. He wrote no scholarly works, and his teaching did not take the typical form of rabbinic commentary on Torah.

   2. He assumed the symbolic world of Kabbalah but taught by means of stories and pointed sayings.

C. The salient elements of Besht's teaching make clear the distinctive development in mysticism he represents.

1. For Besht, all things are filled with God and can reveal God, especially, the human person. This view is known as Panentheism ("There is a presence of God in all things"), which is distinct from Pantheism ("God is all things").
2. Besht expressed great optimism about the human capacity to know and love God and to grow in holiness.
3. In contrast to the Lurianic tradition, he downplayed asceticism and penitence, emphasizing instead the positive feeling of great joy (*simcha*) to be found in worship.
4. Adherence to God (*devequt*) is accomplished more by prayer than by study, and prayer can express itself fully in joyful ecstasy (*hitlahavut*).

III. The Hasidic form of mysticism spread rapidly in Eastern Europe and took on distinct characteristics.

A. Disciples, including the Talmudic scholar Rabbi Dov Baer of Mezritch (1704–1772), joined the movement, which then gained credibility and moved toward the mainstream.
1. Tales centering on the life and character of the Ba'al Shem Tov—his simplicity, compassion, awareness of God, and even his miracles—began to be shaped and disseminated.
2. Hasidic Jews could be found throughout Poland, Russia, Byelorusse, Lithuania, the Ukraine, even in Palestine, in Galilee.

B. The movement also experienced resistance from Jews who regarded it with suspicion and resulted in some excommunications.
1. Rabbi Elijah ben Solomon, the Gaon of Vilna, or the "Great One" of Vilna (1720–1797), although himself a mystic of Kabbalah, fiercely opposed Hasidism.
2. Objections were made, above all, to the relative freedom of the movement from the study of Torah.

C. The focus on the person of Besht led to the emergence of the *tzaddik* in the Hasidic tradition.
1. The *tzaddik* became the center of a community's life as a result of his personality and prayer, rather than his expertise in Law.

2. He was regarded as an exemplar of virtue (and even of the divine life) and considered to have extraordinary qualities.
3. The position of the *tzaddik* was handed down dynastically, at times taking on a messianic coloration.
4. Distinct branches of Hasidism arose because of these dynastic lines, such as the Chabad Lubavitcher.

IV. As it developed historically, both in Europe and in America, the Hasidic movement maintained its distinctive features but also moved closer to the mainline Rabbinic tradition.

    A. The Tzaddik Nachman of Breslav (1772–1810) provides an example of the use of the tale as a teaching instrument.

    B. With Rabbi Menachem Nahum of Chernobyl (1730–1797), we see the cultivation of a life of piety and virtue in Hasidism and the use of the sermon as a means of teaching mystical doctrine.

Recommended Reading:

Buber, M. *Tales of the Hasidim: The Later Masters*.

Questions to Consider:

1. How does the historical development of Hasidism demonstrate the powerful hold of Torah at the center of Jewish consciousness?

2. Discuss the role of stories throughout the Jewish mystical tradition.

Lecture Eleven—Transcript
The Ba'al Shem Tov and the New Hasidism

The rise and fall of Sabbatai Zevi, the mystical Messiah, created the severest sort of crisis for Jewish Mysticism. The Lurianic form of Kabbalism that had spread so widely across the synagogues of Europe now appeared as potentially dangerous. Communities were internally divided between the adherents of Zevi and his opponents. Other Jews resisted any forms of mysticism in favor of the tried-and-true observance of Torah as interpreted through the Talmud. Still others sought a more fundamental reform by abandoning Talmudic tradition altogether in favor of a concentration on the social teaching of the prophets, a topic I will take up in the next presentation. But mysticism is an element in religion that is difficult utterly to suppress or to shame, for it provides the heart of meaning to the exoteric tradition. In this presentation, I consider the last great development in Jewish Mysticism with the Ba'al Shem Tov and the New Hasidism.

It arose in Eastern Europe in the 18th century in circumstances that posed new challenges to Jews. Some of the old ones were still there; the persecution of Jews through pogroms, such as that in 1648, continued sporadically. But Jewish traditional observance was also threatened in a more fundamental way by the Haskalah, the term for the Enlightenment which took place in Europe in this period. For Jews as well as for Christians, the Enlightenment called into question the entire symbolic world of Torah. The Enlightenment made reason the measure of revelation, and reason was defined specifically in terms of scientific reason so that it challenged the very notion of revelation and all it speaks of, a world beyond. And this threatened Judaism in some ways even more than Christianity because of the powerful way in which mystics had inhabited that symbolic world of Torah. A Jewish thinker named Baruch Spinoza (Baruch means "blessing"; his other name is Benedict Spinoza), whose dates are 1632–1677, was one of the first influential critics of the Bible. He was expelled from the synagogue in 1656.

Spinoza tested the stories in the Bible against the measure of the Enlightenment and found those stories to be either historically or scientifically impossible, so he regarded the Bible as not true, and he established a distinction between truth and meaning. The Bible is not true, but it is still meaningful. At the same time, Spinoza's own pantheistic philosophy eerily echoed the world of Kabbalism. He made a distinction between *Natura naturans* and *Natura naturata*, the difference between thought and extension. This sounds an awful lot like *Eyn Sof* and *sefirot* to me. And he considered philosophy to be the long contemplation of the necessary in God, which is possible because of the conquest of the emotions. If you put together this sense of conquering the emotions, contemplating what is necessary in God, and the distinction between *Eyn Sof*—that is to say, thought and extension—we have in Spinoza virtually a secularized version of the Kabbalistic myth.

Another factor is that Sabbatianism continued to divide Jewish communities, and it continues to divide them all the more because of the career of Jacob Frank, whose dates are 1726–1791. One false Messiah was not enough; Jacob Frank appears as a follower of Sabbatai Zevi who also apostatizes, this time, to Christianity. He arose in Polish-dominated Ukraine. He associated with the Sabbatians. He began to proclaim divine revelations that he had received. The Catholic Church gets involved, and Frank and his followers eventually en masse join the Catholic Church in 1759. Again, Jewish rabbis resisted and, at the synod at Brody, excommunicated Jacob Frank and all of his followers. But this was the sort of thing that kept Sabbatianism alive and continued to cause problems for the Jewish community.

A final factor to consider in this context in which Hasidism arose was the difference of circumstances of Jewish life in the Ukraine, where Hasidism began, and in places like Lithuania. In Lithuania, the Talmudic form of Judaism continued to thrive because of the stable conditions and the presence of urban centers, such as Vilna, which could afford to support large synagogues and the study of scholars. In the Ukraine, Jews were scattered in rural villages, and there were no great centers of learning. Hasidism arises in these conditions with a powerful form of popular mysticism that, at the start, centers in the transformation of persons more than the study of texts, focuses more on ecstatic joy than penitential sorrow. We can't understand the Hasidic movement unless we appreciate the charismatic character of its founder, the Rabbi Israel ben Eliezer, who is known as the Ba'al Shem Tov, the "Master of the Good Name," and is abbreviated as "Besht." In the typical Jewish manner of forming acronyms, Ba'al Shem Tov equals Besht.

He was born in 1698 and died in 1760. His early life was that of a simple, relatively uneducated person who was terribly poor, but who was a lover of nature and began to develop profound mystical tendencies. His poverty was acute. He struggled his whole life long simply to make a living, digging ditches, carrying wood. He went through a series of simple occupations, including minding a village tavern. He married, and his wife, Chana, had two children. He served as a helper in the synagogue. He wasn't the rabbi; he wasn't the scholar. He was a lowly helper in the synagogue. He served as a sexton. He rose to the level of a mediator in the Jewish community, helping people resolve disputes. But his special gift and the basis of his fame was that he was a healer. He was somebody who could control the divine name, thus, *Ba'al Shem Tov*. He was the Master of the Good Name. He could inscribe amulets and prescribe herbs, the combination of which would yield healing in sick people. He became known as this pious, poor man who gave help to others through the very practical application of the divine in name. Followers began to be drawn to him. Again, I emphasize the charismatic character of these mystical figures. The Besht began teaching at Medzhybizh around 1740. Even members of the educated elite gathered to hear him teach. He was not a writer. He wrote no scholarly works. His teaching did not take the typical form of rabbinic commentary on Torah.

It's important to recognize that Besht himself inhabited the symbolic world of Kabbalah. Of the very few things that we have of the Ba'al Shem Tov, there is extant a mystical epistle that he wrote to his friend and brother-in-law, and most scholars feel that this is authentic. He says to his brother-in-law:

> On the day of the New Year of the year 5507 [which would be September 1746 C.E.], I engaged in an ascent of the soul, as you know I do, and I saw wondrous things in that vision that I had never before seen since the day I had attained to maturity. That which I saw and learned in my ascent it is impossible to describe or relate even from mouth to mouth. But as I returned to the lower Garden of Eden I saw many souls, both of the living and the dead, those known to me and those unknown. They were more than could be counted and they ran to and fro from world to world through the path provided by that column known to the adepts in the hidden science. They were all in such a state of great rapture that the

mouth would be worn out if it attempted to describe it and the physical ear too indelicate to hear it. ... Their rapture was so great that I resolved to ascend together with them.

Reading this passage in which the Ba'al Shem Tov reports to his brother-in-law what, in fact, had happened to him, we feel that we are still in the realm of Hayyim Vital or of Joseph Karo. It is the world of Merkabah Mysticism, of ascent of the soul. So he does occupy that Kabbalistic world, but he does so not as an interpreter of texts. He did not write commentaries; rather, he taught by means of stories. This becomes important. He told simple tales about the spiritual life and taught by way of aphorism. In effect, Ba'al Shem Tov was a popular teacher of mysticism, rather than a scholarly practitioner of mysticism.

The salient elements of his teaching make clear the distinctive development in Jewish Mysticism that he represents. For Besht, all things are filled with God and can reveal God. It is not simply Torah that is the body and soul of God; everything in nature can also reveal God, and especially, human persons can reveal God. Technically, this view is called Panentheism. It's not Pantheism, "God is all things," but "there is a presence of God in all things." Practically, it approaches a kind of Animism; the world is alive, and magical, and mystical, and God can pop up at any moment in our environment. Secondly, Besht expresses a pronounced optimism about the human capacity to know and to love God and to grow in holiness. He does not emphasize the negative but, rather, the positive. Humans are fundamentally good because God is in them; they can bring the God within them to a greater and greater realization. They do this, thirdly, above all, through the positive feelings of great joy, *simcha*. In contrast to the Lurianic tradition, which so emphasized asceticism and penitence, Ba'al Shem Tov himself emphasized ecstatic joy. Indeed, one of the characteristic expressions of Hasidism is ecstatic dancing and singing, which is an expression of *simcha*, of joy, in the presence of God. So the fourth point is that adherence to God, *devequt*, is found above all in the act of prayer, rather than in the act of study. And prayer can express itself in joyful ecstasy, *hitlahavut*, the ecstatic state of prayer—not only in visions in private but also in public worship.

The Hasidic form of mysticism spread rapidly in Eastern Europe, and it took on distinct characteristics. Many disciples joined, including

Talmudic scholars, such as Rabbi Dov Baer of Mezritch, whose dates are 1704–1772. And when these Talmudic scholars joined the movement, two things happened: One is that the charismatic, spontaneous sort of mysticism of Ba'al Shem Tov tended to move more toward the mainstream, because it would be affected by that Talmudic influx. Secondly, the movement also took on greater credibility. When Talmudic scholars recognized the validity of this form of mysticism, then it becomes mainstream. Tales centering on the life and the character of the Ba'al Shem Tov—his simplicity, his compassion, his awareness of God, and yes, his miracles—began to be shaped and distributed. There's a tremendous focus upon the person of the Ba'al Shem Tov, the holy man, the saint. Hasidic Jews rapidly could be found throughout southeastern Poland, Russia, Byelorusse, Lithuania, the Ukraine, even in Palestine, in Galilee.

As with all such innovations, it also experienced resistance and even excommunication from certain Jews who viewed it with suspicion. Remember the backdrop. We've already experienced Sabbatai Zevi; we've already experienced Jacob Frank. Here's another charismatic figure who seems to privilege individual ecstatic prayer more than Torah. Shouldn't we be suspicious of him and his followers, as well? Does the Ba'al Shem Tov, in other words, represent another disastrous messianic movement? We find resistance to the Ba'al Shem Tov by one of the greatest Talmudic scholars of the age, the Rabbi Elijah ben Solomon, who was called the Gaon of Vilna, or the "Great One" of Vilna. His dates were 1720–1797. The Gaon of Vilna was himself a great mystic in the tradition of Kabbalah. We have a testimony from one of his followers, the Rabbi Hayyim of Volozhin, in which he reports, concerning the Gaon of Vilna:

> "A fortnight ago Thursday, you sat in this place and expounded these and these verses [from Deuteronomy] and Rabbi Simeon ben Yohai [you remember him from the *Zohar*] was sitting at your right hand and the Ari [was sitting] at your left hand." [We have, again, these two great mystics of the past who were present.] Our master was amazed whence this mortal knew all this, and said, "But I remember that on that day I even sent [out] my servant away from the house so that nobody would know." Then our master said to him, "It is true that I expounded awesome mysteries on that occasion," and as he said this his face waxed very pale—which shows that these must have been

truly wonderful things and exalted mysteries, worthy of being expounded in the presence of Simeon ben Yohai. Then our master looked at the dreamer and recognized that he was suffering from melancholia, and melancholics at times have correct and true dreams. Then he ordered his servant to chase the man away.

The following paragraph is the one that is important:

But in truth, all these wonderful things are not wonderful at all in my eyes … for this is Torah and this is its reward. We have a tradition from the *tanna* Rabbi Meir to the effect that he who studies Torah for its own sake "is vouchsafed to many things"—this is a hint at those wonderful things and exalted revelations. And our eyes have seen how all these gifts were fulfilled in our master. … To him, permission was granted to behold the inner light … the most exalted and hidden mysteries … and all the celestial gates were opened to him … as our Sages have said, "He who studies Torah even in distress … the curtain will not be closed before him," for he communes with God [and now the final line], for God and the Torah are one.

This is the tradition of Kabbalah speaking through the Gaon of Vilna, and it was for that very reason that he resisted the Ba'al Shem Tov. He was worried about the relative freedom of this new form of mysticism from the study of Torah and inhabiting the world of Torah.

The concentration on the person of Besht as a holy person led to a distinctive development in Hasidism of a concentration on the figure called the *tzaddik*. The *tzaddik* is not a rabbi. The rabbi is honored in the Jewish community because of a knowledge of Law, the knowledge of Torah, the ability to use midrash in order to instruct the community in how it should live. The *tzaddik* is the center of a community's life, not because of his great learning in Torah but because of his personality and because of his life of prayer. This is really a fundamental shift. In Hasidic communities, the center is the *tzaddik*, and the *tzaddik* is the center because he is a holy person. *Tzaddik* is recognized as an exemplar of virtue, in some cases, even as an embodiment of the divine life. And the *tzaddik* is considered to have extraordinary capacities. We have, for example, a passage from the secret diary that was kept by Rabbi Eizek of Komarno, who was a *tzaddik*, and he says it was on:

> The twentieth day of *Omer*: I was in the town of Dukla. I arrived there in the middle of the night and there was no one to offer me hospitality until a certain tanner invited me into his home. I wanted to recite the night prayers and count the *Omer* but was unable to do so in the home of the tanner [tanners live in a state of uncleanness] so I went to the *bet ha-midrash* [the "house of study"] of the town to pray there. I came to realize the meaning of the descent of the *Shekhinah* and Her anguish as She stood in the street of the tanners. I wept sorely in the presence of the Lord of all because of the anguish of the *Shekhinah*. In my distress, I fainted and slept for a while. I saw a vision of light, a powerful radiance in the form of a virgin all adorned from whose person there came a dazzling light but I was not worthy to see the face. No more of this can be recorded in writing. Her light was brighter than the sun at noonday.

So the *tzaddik* is the one who has these immediate and intimate experiences of mysticism not connected to the study of Torah but connected to the reciting of prayer, to the experience of prayer itself. He recounts that earlier in his life:

> a marvelous light [fell upon him], the *Shekhinah* [was] resting there. This was the first time in my life that I had some little taste of His light, may He be blessed. It was authentic without error or confusion, a wondrous delight and a most pleasant illumination beyond all comprehension. From that time onwards I began to serve the Creator of all with a marvelous unvarying illumination.

So he lived in this state of illumination. Another distinctive feature of Hasidism is that the role of the *tzaddik* is handed down dynastically—that is, from father to son, rather than through, let us say, rabbinic election or selection. There is this sense of holiness, of extraordinary character that is handed on from father to son in specific dynasties, and there are times—and I will mention one in the last lecture in this unit—where a *tzaddik* is even regarded as a messianic figure.

Because of these dynastic lines, distinct branches of Hasidism arose—for example, the Chabad Lubavitcher, which is today the largest group of Hasidic followers. As it developed historically, both in Europe and in America, the Hasidic movement maintained its distinctive features, but it also, perhaps inevitability, moved closer to the mainline rabbinic tradition. Today, Hasidic Jews look very much like the most orthodox of all observers of Talmud; the distinctive elements that were found in the Ba'al Shem Tov have been very much brought within that concentration upon Torah and the observance of Talmud.

There are two figures that I would like to just mention for your reading at the end of this presentation. The first is the Tzaddik Nachman of Breslav, whose dates are 1772–1810. He is one of the great examples of the continuation of the Besht's tradition of teaching through tales, and there is a great collection of his Hasidic tales using stories to teach. For example, he has a story called "The Loss of the Princess." A princess is banished from the court and wanders through the world. A viceroy of the court is sent to bring back the princess and restore her to her position in the court. He experiences many trials and tribulations before he can finally find the princess and bring her back. At a surface reading, this sounds entirely like a simple folktale: A princess is lost, wandered, and is found by a hero. But within the framework of Kabbalistic spirituality, it is the Shekinah that is lost. It is the divine spark that is lost from *Eyn Sof* and wanders in the world. And it is the mystic who must go, find that spark, and return her to her rightful place. These simple-sounding tales are not just charming; they actually teach through metaphor, through indirection, through fable, what the mystical life is about.

The other example I bring to your attention is Rabbi Menachem Nahum of Chernobyl, whose dates are 1730–1797, and with Rabbi Menachem Nahum, we see how Hasidism cultivated a life of piety and virtue and used the sermon as a means of teaching mystical doctrine. We have this wonderful sermon by Menachem on the text from Genesis about two nations being in your womb and two peoples that are going to be set apart. "Because of the sin of Adam and the early generations that followed," Menachem Nahum says, "holy sparks and souls came to be scattered among the nations of the world." You catch what is being said here; this is classic Kabbalism: The divine sparks are being scattered throughout the world because of the sin of Adam. The light is being scattered into the darkness, in this case, into the nations of the world, non-Jews.

> It is through those holy sparks that the nations conduct their affairs; their very life is dependent on them. Without this scattering of sparks they would have no sustenance at all, since all life comes from the Holy.

This is a positive view of non-Jews, of Gentiles. There are divine sparks among all nations. God is present among all people. What is the function of Israel, then?

> This is how it is that proselytes emerge from among the nations, one who has such a holy soul is led to conversion. And that is why Israel have been scattered among the nations: to draw forth those sparks of light.

The role of Israel, cosmically and among nations of the world, is to attract the sparks of light that are among the Gentiles to itself. In this reading, Israel is like *Eyn Sof*, and the sparks among the Gentiles are like the *sefirot*. The role of Israel is to draw these sparks to itself:

> By seeing the awareness that exists in Israel and by believing in the Torah that they have been given, the proselyte draws near. … They have contact with the nations, through commerce or even through words that they exchange [and when that happens], the Jew who has proper faith should be seeking out those holy sparks and drawing them near; he extends himself out to them and raises them upward to their root. For this one needs to have a proper awareness and an honest and whole prayer life. It is this that the messiah is waiting for: that we complete the uplifting of the sparks. When the work is done, life will pass out of the nations and they will no longer exist.

This is a different vision of mending the world. It is that Israel should draw all that is good, all of the righteous Gentiles to itself and, thus, restore the divine light and the people of Israel simultaneously. This is the Messianic Age.

Lecture Twelve
Mysticism in Contemporary Judaism

Scope:

The last 100 years have been tumultuous and tragic for Jews. Conflicts over emancipation and the nature of Jewish identity in the face of modernity led to distinct movements: Reform, Orthodox, and Conservative. Zionism emerged as a secular form of Messianism. The Shoah threatened the very existence of the people, while the State of Israel offered a form of resurrection. What elements of mysticism persist in such an altered tradition? This lecture considers Rabbi Abraham Isaac Kook at the start of this period and touches on contemporary Hasidic communities, popular Kabbalism, and the mystical dimensions in the writings of Abraham Heschel and Martin Buber.

Outline

I. The 19th and 20th centuries severely challenged the capacity of Judaism as a religious tradition to respond to threats, leaving us with, at best, only elements of mysticism in contemporary Judaism. We should note, in particular, four of the threats faced by Judaism.

    A. The emancipation that resulted from the European Enlightenment was a mixed blessing.

        1. Jews were freed from the ghetto and could be citizens but at the cost of assimilation and continuing anti-Semitism.

        2. The Haskalah (Enlightenment) threatened the sacred text of Torah even more profoundly than the Christian Bible because of the premise of Kabbalism with respect to the world and Torah: God and Torah are closely intertwined. The Bible is not simply a text, but it is the world.

    B. The rise of modernity created divisions within Judaism concerning religious identity and practice.

        1. Reform Jews abandoned the Talmudic tradition entirely, focusing instead on the prophets and on social change; temple worship in modern languages resembled Protestantism more than traditional Judaism.

2. Orthodox Jews insisted on maintaining all traditions but tended to equate religious values with cultural ones, not only studying Hebrew for worship but adopting Yiddish as the language of everyday communication and wearing the clothing of the European ghetto, where the Hasidic movement began.

3. Conservative Jews sought a middle ground, continuing the observance of Torah and Talmud as the basis for Jewish life but accepting elements of contemporary culture.

C. Many Jews responded to continuing persecution by embracing Zionism, the hope for a Jewish homeland, which began with Moses Hess (1812–1875).

1. The religious dimension of Zionism was mixed; at times, it appeared to be a completely secular enterprise.

2. Return to *Eretz Israel* by political means affected messianic expectations.

D. The most fundamental challenge was posed by the Shoah (Holocaust), which took place in Nazi Germany between 1932 and 1945, affecting the foundation of Jewish conviction with the systematic murder of 6 million Jews.

1. For some, like Richard Rubenstein, religious belief and messianic hope were destroyed.

2. For others, such as Emil Fackenheim, the State of Israel itself is envisaged as the Messianic Age, the resurrection of the people.

3. For some, such as Holocaust survivor Elie Wiesel, the experience of the Shoah demanded a response of silent witness and the cautious recovery of the threads of meaning.

II. Traditional forms of Jewish Mysticism continue to be represented in the contemporary world.

A. Familiar to many Americans (especially through the work of Chaim Potok) is the Hasidic dynasty known as Chabad Lubavitch, based primarily in Brooklyn and distinguished by its unique customs.

1. With more than 200,000 adherents, it is among the largest sects deriving from the movement begun by the Ba'al Shem Tov. Its origins can be traced to the Russian town of Lyubavichi and the figure of Scneur Zalman of

Liadi. This movement follows the principles of Lurianic Kabbalism and the piety of the Ba'al Shem Tov.

    2. The acronym Chabad represents "wisdom" (*chochmah*), "understanding" (*binah*), and "knowledge" (*da'at*); while maintaining the emotional fervor of Hasidism, it emphasizes the role of the mind and learning.

    3. The seventh rebbe in the dynasty, Menachem Mendel Schneerson, who was leader from 1950–1994, is particularly important, regarded by some as a messianic figure.

    4. The sect is energetically missionary, seeking in a variety of ways to bring other Jews into Orthodox observance.

B. A great 20th-century mystic in the classical mold was Rabbi Abraham Isaac Kook (1865–1935), the chief rabbi of Palestine before the establishment of the State of Israel.

    1. Born in the Latvian village of Grieve, he served congregations in Latvia, Gaza, and London before becoming chief rabbi of the entire Jewish community in Palestine, a position recognized by Jews throughout the world.

    2. In a distinctive fashion, he combined orthodoxy, Orthodox Mysticism, Zionism, and liberalism, including an openness to contemporary thought.

    3. His *Lights of Penitence* shows his appropriation of a deeply traditional theme in a fresh fashion.

    4. Similarly, he makes available in a clear and attractive manner the insights of Kabbalah.

III. In both popular and scholarly forms, Jewish Mysticism continues to exercise influence even outside the Jewish community.

A. Kabbalism has taken on a life of its own as one version of contemporary spirituality, attractive to those searching for meaning in a secular culture.

    1. Kabbalism centers offer instruction in meditation and prayer, without any necessary connection to the observance of the Law or even Jewish convictions.

    2. Kabbalah.com is an Internet site that perfectly represents the world of pop spirituality: The site's main attraction is that it sells the red string worn around the wrist to ward off the evil eye.

B. The scholarly study of Jewish Mysticism has generated intense interest in the riches of this spiritual tradition.

  1. In 1938, Gershom Scholem delivered the lectures that became *Major Trends in Jewish Mysticism*, opening a field of investigation into an area earlier critical scholars had scorned.

  2. The research of many successors has led to the editing, publication, and translation of mystical texts of great significance and power.

C. Martin Buber and Abraham Heschel are two Jewish thinkers who are, perhaps, more famous in the Gentile world than among their fellow Jews; both were deeply marked by the mystical tradition.

  1. Martin Buber (1878–1965) was a philosopher and Zionist who broke from Jewish life and studied continental philosophy; he edited and translated Hasidic tales. In *I and Thou*, he develops an understanding of human existence as an experience of encounter and dialogue, as well as one of calculation and manipulation.

  2. Abraham Joshua Heschel (1907–1972) received Talmudic training and a secular doctorate from the University of Berlin. A Conservative Jew, he taught Jewish Ethics and Mysticism at the Jewish Theological Seminary. A civil rights activist, he wrote works that brought Jewish insight to the larger world, including *The Prophets*, *The Sabbath*, and *God in Search of Man*.

D. The present is a time when the "sparks of light" of the Jewish mystical tradition are scattered in many directions; the question of whether or how they can be gathered again into a unified form remains unclear.

E. What seems certain is that if mysticism is to be authentically, genuinely Jewish, it must involve deep study and devotion to the world of Torah and the God therein.

Recommended Reading:

Bokser, B. Z., trans. *Abraham Isaac Kook* (*Classics of Western Spirituality*.)

Questions to Consider:

1. What sense is there to a Kabbalism disconnected from the study of Torah and the observance of the Commandments?

2. How do the qualities shown by a figure such as Rabbi Abraham Isaac Kook offer a way forward for Jewish spirituality?

Lecture Twelve—Transcript
Mysticism in Contemporary Judaism

Jewish Mysticism is by far the oldest and the longest lasting of the three traditions that we study in this course. We've seen that it has been marked by great flexibility in form and expression, together with an equally impressive stability and focus. It is about Torah from beginning to end and how the living God is revealed in Torah. In this final lecture of the unit on Judaism, however, we can speak at best only of elements of mysticism in contemporary Judaism. This is because the 19th and 20th centuries challenged the capacity of Judaism as a religious tradition to respond to unparalleled threats. Four of them in particular need to be noted.

The first is that of Jewish political emancipation that came about as a result of the European Enlightenment, in the U.S.A. in 1789, freedom of worship in France in 1791. It proved to be a mixed blessing. Jews were freed from the ghetto, to be sure, and could participate in the larger life of society as citizens, but they faced two continuing threats. The first was the threat of assimilation. Once they were liberated into the wider society, the attractions of marriage into Gentile families proved irresistible for many Jews, and Judaism has suffered a steady loss in numbers due to assimilation into the Gentile world. But on the other side, there was, if anything, continuing or even increased anti-Semitism. It is, after all, one of the paradoxes of modernity that everybody is acceptable as long as they are the same. If you persist in remaining really different, as Jewish communities traditionally remain really different, you continue to be despised and not accepted. And Jews became vividly aware of this in the Dreyfus Affair and became aware of the fact that Jews continued not to be safe, continued to be subject to anti-Semitism, even though they enjoyed civic liberty. The Haskalah, furthermore, which I mentioned in the last lecture, is the Jewish term for the Enlightenment, threatened the sacred text of Torah even more than the Christian Bible because of the premise of Kabbalism with respect to the world and Torah. God and Torah are closely intertwined. The Bible is not simply a text, but it is the world.

The rise of modernity created divisions within Judaism concerning religious identity and practice, and these divisions concerned precisely how Jews should respond to the dramatic demystification of the world that took place in the Enlightenment. Reform Jews abandoned the Talmudic tradition entirely. The reform began in Germany, and in America is symbolized by the Pittsburgh Platform of 1885. That platform said that the Talmud is no longer the basis of Jewish life; rather, there was a focus on the prophets of Israel—not the Law but the prophets—and their call to social justice. Judaism aligned itself with a sort of a vision of Messianism which was incremental social progress. Temple worship in modern languages made Jewish worship resemble Protestantism more than traditional Judaism. In fact, it was no longer called the synagogue but, rather, temple.

Orthodox Jews, in contrast, insisted on maintaining traditions, but because maintenance of traditions takes place in a world in which everything else has changed inevitably, the Orthodox tradition appears somewhat reactionary. There is not only a clinging to religious values but an equation of religious values with cultural customs; not only the study of Hebrew in worship but the use of Yiddish as the language of communication within the community; and the wearing of the clothing of European ghettos, where the Hasidic movement began. In Orthodoxy, there is the maintenance of the observance of Talmud, the study of Talmud in Hebrew, but the cultural value assigned to Yiddish, and clothing, and so forth marks Orthodox Jews as even more different within contemporary society.

A middle ground was sought by Conservative Jews, whose main social location was the Jewish Theological Seminary in New York, which was founded in 1886. This middle ground was to continue to observe Torah and Talmud as the basis for Jewish life but without the accoutrements of European ghetto existence, so one could accept elements of contemporary culture. By far today, Conservative Jews are the smallest body, and Orthodox and Reform Jews are the main ones that most people come in contact with.

The third factor at work here is the development of Zionism. Many Jews responded to the reality of continuing persecution by embracing Zionism, the hope for a Jewish homeland. This began especially with Moses Hess, whose dates are 1812–1875, and became an organization under Theodore Herzl in 1897. This is somewhat correlated to the Dreyfus Affair, this sense that no place is safe for Jews except their own homeland. The organization was founded to seek a Jewish homeland, and the focus became on Palestine or *Eretz Israel* as the place of safety for Jews. But the religious dimension of

Zionism was always mixed. Sometimes it appeared to religious Jews as a completely secular enterprise. Herzl simply declared, "The Jews are a nation." And the return to *Eretz Israel* not led by a Messiah but, rather, accomplished through political means obviously changed perceptions of what that event meant.

The fourth and most fundamental challenge was posed by the Shoah, the Holocaust, that took place in Nazi Germany between 1932–1945, when the entire frame of Jewish conviction was challenged by the deaths of 6 million Jews, who were systematically murdered for no other reason than that they were Jews. For some, like Richard Rubenstein in his book *After Auschwitz*, religious belief and messianic hope were destroyed. Rubenstein offers a version of the death-of-God theology specifically with respect to the experience of Auschwitz. Remember the Jewish messianic conviction that when things got bad enough, the Messiah would come, God would intervene. Rubenstein said, "Well, the deaths of 6 million Jews seems to be an event large enough," and the non-appearance of the Messiah put into question all of this traditional belief about the relationship between God and Israel and the way that the living God would protect Israel when it was most in danger of being destroyed.

For others, such as Emil Fackenheim, the Canadian Jewish philosopher, in his book *The Jewish Bible After the Holocaust*, the State of Israel is envisaged as the Messianic Age, the resurrection of the people. And the whole point of being Jewish is not to look for an afterlife but to look to protect Jewish children. For Fackenheim, this demands an entirely new way of reading the Bible. The center of the Bible for Fackenheim is the book of Esther, where God is never mentioned, but where Jews fight against tyranny to protect their own people. And the Bible should be read, says Fackenheim, as a *folks Geschichte*, as the history of this people, as a historical narrative, rather than in terms of mysticism, which distracts us from the harsh realities of life in this world in which Jews are always subject to violence and extermination.

For some, the experience of the Shoah demanded silent witness and the very cautious recovery of the threads of meaning. This position is found, above all, in the Holocaust survivor Elie Wiesel, who has written stunningly powerful works on his own experience in Auschwitz but also has written works of slow and cautious encouragement about the recovery of meaning. In the introduction to his book *The Gates of the Forest*, Wiesel begins with a Hasidic tale:

> When the great Rabbi Israel Ba'al Shem Tov saw misfortune threatening the Jews it was his custom to go into a certain part of the forest to meditate. There he would light a fire, [and] say a special prayer, and the miracle would be accomplished and the misfortune averted. Later, when his disciple, the celebrated Magid of Mezritch, had occasion, for the same reason, to intercede with heaven, he would go to the same place in the forest and say: "Master of the Universe, listen! I do not know how to light the fire, but I am still able to say the prayer." And again the miracle would be accomplished. Then it fell to Rabbi Israel of Ryzhyn to overcome misfortune. Sitting in his armchair, his head in hands, he spoke to God: "I am unable to light the fire and [I] do not know the prayer; I cannot even find the place in the forest. All I can do is to tell the story, and this must be sufficient." And it was sufficient.

And Wiesel concludes the story: "God made man because he loves stories." The basic response to the Holocaust, then, is to continue to tell the story.

Despite these cataclysmic challenges to Jewish identity and life, traditional forms of Jewish Mysticism continue to be represented in the contemporary world. Familiar to many Americans in particular, especially through the novels of Chaim Potok, such as *My Name Is Asher Lev*, and the movies based upon those novels—most familiar is the Hasidic dynasty known as Chabad Lubavitch, which was derived from the Ba'al Shem Tov in a very early period of Hasidism. It is based primarily in Brooklyn and is distinguished by its distinctive customs. With over 200,000 adherents, it is among the largest sects deriving from the movement begun by the Ba'al Shem Tov, with an origin in the Russian town of Lyubavichi and with a beginning marked by Schneur Zalman of Liadi. It follows the principles of Lurianic Kabbalism, together with the piety of the Ba'al Shem Tov. If "Lubavitcher" comes from the hometown of the dynasty, the term "Chabad" is a typical Hebrew acronym. It comes from the term "wisdom," *chochmah*; "understanding," *binah*; and "knowledge," *da'at*. What this indicates, Chabad, is that while this movement or dynasty within Hasidism maintains the emotional fervor of Hasidism, including such things as ritual dancing and singing and ecstatic prayer, it also emphasizes the role of the mind in learning and study—understanding, wisdom, knowledge.

The seventh rebbe, as they are called—the rebbe rather than rabbi—in the Lubavitcher dynasty, Menachem Mendel Schneerson, served as head of this community for an astonishingly long period, 44 years, in Brooklyn from 1950–1994. And he is a particularly important figure, because by some within the Lubavitcher movement, he is regarded as a messianic figure. And we can see beginning to accrue around the figure of this rebbe, who has now died, some of the similar kinds of expectations that gathered around the figure of Sabbatai Zevi. This group of Hasidic Jews is energetically missionary; it actively seeks proselytes and to bring not only Gentiles but other Jews into Orthodox observance of the Talmud. Characteristic of many conservative religious movements in today's world, they are amazingly up to date in matters of technology. They have Bible camps and all of these sorts of things, like evangelical Christians do, to try to strengthen the adherence of members and to draw new members.

Quite a different example of the continuation of Jewish Mysticism in the 20th century is the great Rabbi Abraham Isaac Kook, whose dates are 1865–1935, the chief rabbi of Palestine prior to the establishment of the State of Israel. He was born in the Latvian village of Grieve. He served congregations in Latvia, Gaza, and London before becoming the chief rabbi of the entire Jewish community in Palestine, a position he held from 1921–1935, and was recognized by Jews throughout the world. Kook was distinctive in the manner in which he combined orthodoxy and Orthodox Mysticism, Zionism, and liberalism, including a remarkable openness to contemporary thought. In his work the *Lights of Penitence*, he shows how he appropriates a deeply traditional theme in a fresh fashion. He says,

> Penitence is, in essence, an effort to return to one's original status, to the source of life and higher being in their fullness, without limitation and diminution, in their highest spiritual character, as illumined by the simple, radiant divine light. ["Simple, radiant, divine light"—we're in the realm of Kabbalism.] The life process lowers us to proliferating fragmentation [scattering], which tends to solidify our limited existence, the more it reaches out and becomes

involved in action, in undertakings and accomplishments. This creates the impression that our lives are firm and stable. It is for this reason that we feel weak and failing as the will prods us to return to the primary source that transcends all its proliferating particularities. As a result of this weakening of the will, even our spiritual aspiration is weakened.

He continues:

As we ascend on the ladder of penitence, we must also hold on to the practical particularizations, with their stirrings, the thoughts and strivings they conjure up, and raise them as well together with the ascent of our inner being toward the divine, to be reunited with our original source. However life breaks down into particularization, it continues to draw light from the original divine light, and it needs to return to the higher realm, together with the essence of our souls.

This is a new and fresh fashion, a restatement of the convictions of Lurianic Kabbalism about the scattering of the divine sparks and the need to bring them back together.

Even more striking are the words of Rabbi Kook on the doctrine of evolution. He says:

The doctrine of evolution that is presently gaining acceptance in the world has a greater affinity with the secret teachings of the Cabbalah than all other philosophies. Evolution, which proceeds on a course of improvement, offers us the basis of optimism in the world. How can we despair when we realize that everything evolves and improves? In probing the inner meaning of evolution toward an improved state, we find here an explanation of the divine concepts with absolute clarity. It is precisely the *Eyn Sof* in action that manages to bring to realization the infinite potentiality. Evolution sheds light on all the ways of God. All existence evolves and ascends, as this may be discerned in some of its parts. Its ascent is general, as is its particulars. It ascends toward the heights of the absolute good. Obviously the good and the comprehensive all go together.

Please remember this; we'll hear something very similar in the Christian mystic Teilhard de Chardin.

No particularity will remain outside, not a spark will be lost from the ensemble. All will share in the climatic culmination. Toward this objective one needs to be sensitized spiritually to seek God on a higher plane. This is effected through service of faith in God.

Here we have an Orthodox Jewish rabbi deeply steeped in Kabbalism who is able to embrace the theory of evolution as precisely corresponding to the great mystic hopes of the centuries.

In both popular and scholarly forms, furthermore, Jewish Mysticism continues to exercise influence even outside the Jewish community. Kabbalism has taken on a life of its own as one version of contemporary spirituality which is attractive to those searching for meaning in a secular culture. Celebrities like Madonna and Britney Spears attend Kabbalism centers that offer instruction in meditation and prayer without, however, any necessary connection to the observance of Talmud or even Jewish convictions. Even more interesting is the Internet site Kabbalah.com, a site that perfectly represents the world of pop spirituality; the main attraction that I could see was the ability to purchase the red string that one could wear around one's wrist as a way of warding off the evil eye. Kabbalah.com is a long distance from the serious study of Torah undertaken by traditional Jewish Mysticism.

Another way in which Jewish Mysticism continues, even among Gentiles, is the scholarly study of Jewish Mysticism, which has generated an intense interest in the riches of this spiritual tradition. It was only in 1938 that Gershom Scholem delivered the lectures that became his book *Major Trends in Jewish Mysticism*, which opened up an entire field of investigation into an area that earlier critical scholars had simply scorned. Even within the great tradition of Jewish historiography, mysticism was regarded as something that was somehow not totally worthy of attention. Gershom Scholem brought this remarkable history to everybody's attention, and the research of many successors has led to the editing, and the publication, and the translation of mystical texts of great significance and power. This unit of this course would have been totally impossible, for example, without the series called *The Classics of Western Spirituality*, which has published so many of the primary texts of the Jewish Kabbalistic tradition.

I would like to conclude by looking at a couple of Jewish thinkers who have addressed the Gentile world and perhaps are even more famous in the Gentile world than among their fellow Jews, both of whom were deeply marked by the mystical tradition. The first is Martin Buber, whose dates are 1878–1965. He's a philosopher; he's an active Zionist. He broke from the traditions of Jewish life in his young manhood and studied continental philosophy. In the course of his life, he began to be fascinated by Hasidic tales, and he began to edit and translate them. And in his later writings, such as his most significant book, *I and Thou*, he develops an understanding of human existence as one of encounter and dialogue, as well as of calculation and manipulation. Buber is a powerful critic of the world which reduces everything to I and it. He calls for virtually a mystical approach to relationships among persons, including the person of a higher order. We read in Buber:

> The *Thou* meets me through grace—it is not found by seeking. But my speaking of the primary word to it is an act of my being, is indeed *the* act of my being. The *Thou* meets me. But I step into direct relation with it. Hence the relation means being chosen and choosing, suffering and action in one, just as any action of the whole being, which means the suspension of all partial actions, and consequently of all sensations of actions grounded only in their particular limitation, is bound to resemble suffering. The primary word *I—Thou* can be spoken only with the whole being. Concentration and fusion into the whole being can never take place through my agency, nor can it ever take place without me. I become through my relation to the *Thou*; as I become *I*, I say *Thou*. All real living is meeting.

This never mentions the word God, never refers to Torah, but it is a form of appreciation for the dimensions of life that is profoundly marked by the Jewish mystical tradition and, specifically, of Hasidism.

The second figure is Abraham Joshua Heschel, whose dates are 1907–1972. He received Talmudic training, as well as a secular doctorate, from the University of Berlin. He was a Conservative Jew who taught Jewish Ethics and Mysticism at the Jewish Theological Seminary. He was a civil rights activist in the 1960s, and he wrote a number of books that brought the insights of the Jewish tradition and, particularly, of Jewish Mysticism to the larger world. Among those are his books called *The Prophets*, *The Sabbath*, and interestingly, *God in Search of Man* (not humans in search of God but *God in Search of Man*).

This is a period when the sparks of light of the Jewish mystical tradition are scattered in many directions. It's not entirely clear whether or how they can be gathered together again in a unified form. What seems certain is that if mysticism is to be authentically, genuinely Jewish, it must involve the deep study and devotion to the world of Torah and of the God disclosed by Torah. I want to close this unit with the words of a Hasidic master of the 20th century, Aaron Roth, who wrote in his essay "Agitation of the Soul" in 1934 these simple words:

> Now the Holy One, blessed be He, the Torah and Israel are one. For the light of His holy name, blessed be He, resides in the letters of the Torah and when a man moves his lips in holiness and adheres with all the power of his thought an inwardness of heart to the innermost light of the holy letters, he then becomes a veritable palace [*hekal*] and sanctuary [or temple] for the holy *Shekhinah*, provided that he has this in mind.

Timeline

B.C.E.

c. 1800..Abraham.

c. 1300..Moses and the Exodus.

8th century...................................Isaiah, Hoshea.

7th–6th centuries ....Jeremiah, Exile, Ezekiel.

323 ....Death of Alexander the Great.

c. 167–164..................................Book of Daniel.

1st century...................................Essene community at Qumran.

C.E.

c. 28–31.......................................Ministry and crucifixion of Jesus.

c. 33–64.......................................Paul's ministry and correspondence.

c. 50..Death of Philo of Alexandria.

64 ....Persecution under Nero.

68–100..Gospels and other New Testament compositions.

70 ....Destruction of the Temple in Jerusalem.

96 ....Persecution of Christians under Domitian.

c. 115..Martyrdom of Ignatius of Antioch.

135 ....Bar Kochba Revolt, destruction of Jerusalem, martyrdom of Rabbi Akiva.

c. 135–155..................................Marcion and Valentinus flourish (Gnosticism).

c. 160–225..................................Irenaeus and Tertullian flourish.

c. 184–254..................................Life of Origen of Alexandria.

c. 200..Mishnah composed by Judah ha-Nasi.

251–356.....................................Antony of Egypt.

4th century.................................Compilation of the Talmud of the Land of Israel.

303 ....Great Persecution of Christians under Diocletian.

313 ....Constantine issues the Edict of Milan.

325 ....Ecumenical Council at Nicea.

c. 332–395.................................Gregory of Nyssa.

345–399.....................................Evagrius Ponticus.

347–407.....................................Life of John Chrysostom, great preacher and theologian in the Orthodox tradition.

354–430.....................................Life of Augustine of Hippo.

c. 360–c. 430 ....Palladius and John Cassian, who write of desert monks.

381 ....Council of Constantinople under Theodosius I, theological dominance of the Cappadocians (Gregory, Basil, Gregory).

5th–6th centuries ....Compilation of the Babylonian Talmud, Pseudo-Dionysius (the Aereopagite).

451 ....Council at Chalcedon: Two Natures in Christ.

c. 525..Benedict of Nursia founds a monastery at Monte Cassino, writes the *Rule for Monks*.

532–537.....................................Great church of Hagia Sophia constructed in Constantinople.

c. 540–604.................................Gregory I (the Great), bishop of Rome, pope 590–604.

570–632.....................................Life of the Prophet Muhammad.

c. 579–c. 649 ....John Climacus, abbot at Mount Sinai.

c. 580–662................................Maximus the Confessor, defender of Orthodoxy in the monotheite controversy.

610 ....Muhammad begins recitation of the Qur'an.

622 ....Hijrah, emigration to Medina, first year of Islamic dating.

632–661...................................Orthodox caliphate.

641–725...................................Islamic expansion across North Africa to France.

661–751...................................Umayyad caliphate.

726 ....Iconoclastic Controversy in Eastern Orthodoxy.

732 ....Charles Martel defeats Muslim forces at Tours.

742–814...................................Charlemagne, Holy Roman Emperor.

750–1258.................................'Abbasid Caliphate.

801 ....Death of Rabi'a al-'Adawiyya, female Sufi.

873 ....Disappearance (or death) of the 12th imam.

874 ....Death of Abu Yazid al-Bistami, early Sufi.

910 ....Death of al-Junayd, early Sufi.

922 ....Death of Mansur al-Hallaj, Sufi "heretic."

c. 936.......................................Death of early Sufi theologian Abu'l-Hasan al-Ash'ari.

942 ....Death of great scholar Saadia Gaon.

c. 950	Death of al-Farabi, Arabic philosopher.
988	Death of Abu Nasr as-Sarraj, early Sufi.
1006–1089	Khwaja Abdullah Ansari, Persian Sufi.
1037	Death of Ibn Sina, Arabic philosopher.
1054	Schism between Eastern (Greek) and Western (Latin) churches.
1058–1111	Al-Ghazzali, theologian, philosopher, Sufi.
1085–1148	William of St. Thierry, associate of Bernard, scriptural interpreter.
1088–1167	Founding of the universities at Bologna, Paris, and Oxford.
1090–1153	Bernard of Clairvaux, founder of the Cistercian order of monks.
1095–1099	First Crusade against the "infidels."
1098–1179	Hildegard of Bingen, Benedictine visionary.
1100–1160	Peter Lombard, beginnings of Scholasticism in universities.
1135–1204	Moses Maimonides.
1150–1250	Hasidei Ashkenazi—German "Pious/Devout."
c. 1160–1235	Isaac ben Abraham (Isaac the Blind), early Kabbalist.
1165–1240	Ibn al-'Arabi, poet and Sufi visionary.
1170–1221	St. Dominic, founder of the "Order of Preachers" (Dominicans).

1173	Death of Richard of St. Victor, student of mysticism.
1181–1235	'Umar ibn al-Farid, Egyptian Sufi poet.
1181/82–1226	Francis of Assisi, founder of the Franciscans (mendicants).
1193–1254	Clare of Assisi, founder of Poor Clares.
1198	Death of Ibn Rushd, Arabic philosopher.
1202–1204	Fourth Crusade, sacking of Constantinople.
1207–1273	Jalal ad-Din Rumi, great Sufi poet in Persian.
1208–1282/94	Mechtilde of Magdeburg, Beguine mystic.
1213–1289	Fakhruddin Iraqi, Persian Sufi poet.
c. 1221–1274	Bonaventure, biographer of Francis and mystic.
1225–1274	Thomas Aquinas, great Scholastic theologian.
1240–c.1291	Abraham of Abulafia, prophetic Kabbalist.
1242–1325	Nizam ad-Din Awliya, Persian Sufi master.
1250–1309	Ibn 'Ata'illah, third *shaykh* of the Shadhiliyyah order.
1258–1924	Ottoman Caliphate.
c. 1260–1328	Meister Eckhardt, Dominican mystic.
1263–1381	Sharafuddin Maneri, Indian Sufi master.

1265–1321	Life of Dante, author of *The Divine Comedy*.
1296–1359	Gregory Palamas, advocate of Hesychasm.
1300–1349	Richard Rolle of Hampole, English mystic.
1300–1361	Johannes Tauler, disciple of Eckhardt.
1300–1366	Henry Suso, Dominican mystic.
1303–1373	Birgitta, visionary from Sweden.
1305	Death of Moses de León, author of the *Zohar*.
1330–1384	John Wycliffe, English reformer and translator of the Bible.
1330–1400	English mystics flourish (Julian, Rolle, Hilton).
1332–1390	Ibn 'Abbad of Ronda, Sufi master of North Africa.
c. 1342/43–1400	Geoffrey Chaucer, author of *The Canterbury Tales*.
1342–c. 1416	Julian of Norwich, English anchoress and mystic.
1343–1396	Walter Hilton, English mystic.
1347–1380	Catherine of Siena, Italian mystic.
c. 1373–c. 1440	Margery Kempe, English mystic and autobiographer.
1380–1471	Thomas à Kempis, author of *Imitation of Christ*.
1453	Constantinople falls to Turkish Muslims; the age of exploration begins.
1483–1546	Martin Luther, German reformer.

1484–1531.................................Ulrich Zwingli, Swiss reformer.

1488–1575.................................Safed spirituality: Karo, Cordovero, Luria.

1489–1556.................................Thomas Cranmer, key figure in establishing the Church of England and leading author of the *Book of Common Prayer* (1549).

1492 ....Expulsion of the Jews from Catholic Spain.

c. 1492–c. 1540 ....Francisco de Osuna, Spanish mystic.

1509–1564.................................John Calvin, French reformer.

1515–1582.................................Teresa of Ávila, mystic and reformer of the Carmelites.

1517 ....Luther's Ninety-Five Theses.

1534 ....Divorce of Henry VIII, beginning of the Church of England.

1540 ....Jesuits founded by Ignatius of Loyola to defend faith and the pope.

1542–1591.................................John of the Cross, mystic and reformer of the Carmelites.

1545–1563.................................Council of Trent.

1555–1621.................................Johann Arndt, author of *True Christianity*.

1575–1624.................................Jakob Boehme, German Lutheran mystic.

1582 ....Congregationalist churches in England.

1596–1650.................................René Descartes, French philosopher who, with the British philosophers Locke and Hume, anticipated the Enlightenment and Deism.

1612 ....Baptist churches in England.

1613–1667	Jeremy Taylor, Anglican spiritual writer.
1626	Death of Isaiah Horowitz, author of *The Two Tablets of the Covenant*.
1626–1676	Sabbatai Zevi.
1635–1705	Philipp Jakob Spener, founder of German Pietism.
1686–1761	William Law, Anglican spiritual writer.
1698–1760	Israel ben Eliezer (also called the Ba'al Shem Tov, "Master of the Good Name").
1703–1791	John Wesley, with his brother Charles (1707–1788), founds the Methodists in England and America.
1703–1792	Muhammad al-Wahhab, Islamic reformer.
1726–1750	Great Awaking in America.
1726–1791	Jacob Frank.
1749–1809	Nicodemos of the Holy Mountain, Hesychast.
1776	American Declaration of Independence.
1789	French Revolution.
1799–1877	August Tholuck, pastor in the German Awakening.
1859	Death of Muhammad ibn 'Ali al-Sanusi, Algerian Islamic reformer.
1865–1935	Abraham Isaac Kook.
1869–1870	First Vatican Council (papal infallibility).
1869–1934	Ahmad al-Alawi, Algerian Sufi.

1877–1938....................................Muhammad Iqbal, Islamic modernist.

1878–1965....................................Martin Buber.

1881–1955....................................Teilhard de Chardin.

1891–1978....................................Fatima al-Yashrutiyya, Palestinian Sufi.

1907–1972....................................Abraham Heschel.

1909–1943....................................Simone Weil.

1915–1968....................................Thomas Merton.

1924–1996....................................Idries Shah, advocate of universal Sufism.

1962–1965....................................Second Vatican Council.

Glossary

allegory: A method of interpreting (especially) sacred texts for a deeper, esoteric meaning, as when the Song of Solomon is understood as referring to the love between God and Israel.

almsgiving: The sharing of possessions; in one fashion or another, a required element in all three religious traditions.

anchorite: From the Greek *anachorein*, "to withdraw," a man (the female is "anchoress") who lives as a hermit; in the Middle Ages, anchorites were sometimes walled into chapels or churches.

apocalyptic: From the Greek "out from hiding," a literature or worldview based on a vision of heaven and/or the future.

apocrypha: From the Greek for "hidden things," the term refers to books not included in the Jewish or Christian canon of Scripture.

apophasis: In orthodox theology, affirmation through negation, such as "God is not good" (in the manner humans understand goodness).

apostle: Literally, "one sent on a commission"; used of early Christian leaders, such as Paul, and sometimes used to translate *rasul* for Muhammad.

asceticism: From the Greek *askesis*, or "discipline," a disciplined way of life that emphasizes the rejection of physical pleasure and possessions, as well as the control of the passions.

Besmillah: The short statement preceding every sura of the Qur'an: "In the name of Allah, the compassionate, the merciful."

Christology: The understanding of the person and work of Jesus Christ. Differences in this doctrine caused major conflicts in Christianity from the 4th to the 7th centuries.

cenobite: From Greek *koinos bios* ("common life"), monks of the West, especially following the Rule of Benedict, who live a life of full community; includes both male and female houses.

Constantinople: The "New Rome" founded by the Christian emperor Constantine in the 4th century; center for the Byzantine Empire and named Istanbul when conquered by the Turks.

creed: From the Latin, *credo*, "I believe," a formal statement of belief; Christians recite either the Apostles' Creed or the Nicene Creed in worship. Muslims recite the *shahadah*.

Crusades: Between the 11th and 15th centuries, a series of military expeditions undertaken by Christian rulers and popes in an effort to wrest control of the Holy Land from Muslims.

dervish: In Sufism, a wandering beggar; the "whirling dervishes" are those in a state of ecstasy during the *samas*, the song and dance associated especially with the Mawlawi order.

dhikr: The Sufi mode of "recollection" in prayer, often involving the telling of the names of Allah and, in some orders, the simple name of Allah itself.

esoteric: From the Greek for "within," the inner or secret meaning or significance of texts or rituals, favored especially by mystics.

Essenes: The separatist Jewish sect at the Dead Sea whose scrolls reveal a devotion to Torah and distinct mystical tendencies.

Eucharist: The Christian sacrament of the Lord's Supper; in the medieval period, the conviction that the body and blood of Christ were truly present in the host made the Eucharist an ontological link to union with Christ.

exoteric: From the Greek for "outside," the outer and public understanding of texts and rituals within a religious community.

Eyn Sof (or *Ein-Sof*): In Kabbalism, the divine in itself, distinct from all existents though the source of all existent things.

fana: The next-to-highest state in Sufi Mysticism, "annihilation" or "passing away"; the loss of the self in Allah.

fana al-fana: The highest state in Sufi Mysticism, "passing away of passing away"; a state of union with Allah that "abides."

gematria: The practice of deriving mystical meaning from the fact that the Hebrew letters are also numbers, so that combinations of letters have both numerical and semantic value. Found in Kabbalah and in the Prophetic Kabbalism of Abraham Abulafia.

ghazal: A love song (also called *diwan*), used in some Sufi poetry to express the love of the mystic for Allah.

gnosis: In Greek, "knowledge," used especially for knowledge that is nonempirical or revealed. In all three traditions, the approach to God through the mind; in Christianity, the heretical movement of the 2nd and 3rd centuries is called Gnosticism.

Hadith: Stories about the Prophet that were passed on after his death by associates, often containing authoritative statements, and one of the important sources for the Shari'ah.

Hajj: Pilgrimage to Mecca, which is one of the five Pillars of Islam and is required of Muslims who are physically and financially able to make the pilgrimage once in a lifetime. The Hajj climaxes in the common prayer on the Plain of Arafat.

hanyf: "Righteous man," applied to Abraham, who was neither Jew nor Christian yet was submissive to Allah.

Hasidism: The "Pious/Devout"; used in the Jewish mystical tradition for the *Hasidei Askenazi* of medieval Germany and the followers of the Ba'al Shem Tov in the 18th century.

Hekaloth: In Jewish Mysticism of the Rabbinic period, the heavenly palaces within which the presence of God is to be found; from *hekal*, "palace."

hermit: An individual who lives in complete solitude to devote his or her life to prayer. The form of asceticism associated with Antony of Egypt.

Hesychasm: From the Greek *hesychia*, "silence" or "quiet," the contemplative prayer associated especially with Eastern orthodoxy; makes use of the "Jesus Prayer."

Hijrah: The flight or emigration of Muhammad and his followers ("the emigrants") in 622 C.E. from Mecca to Medina. The Hijrah marks the start of the Islamic dating system because of its symbolic importance in the success of the Islamic movement.

Holy Spirit: The power from God that was active in biblical prophets that Christians associated especially to the resurrection of Jesus; the "third person" of the Christian Trinity (along with Father and Son).

icon: From the Greek *eikon*, "image," a pictorial representation of Christ or a saint; devotion expressed through such icons was a staple of Hesychastic piety.

iconoclastic: Literally, the breaking of icons or images. Islam was aniconic—it did not allow representations of Allah—and Orthodox rulers in the context of Islam agitated for the elimination of icons in Byzantium. John of Damascus was the champion of the Orthodox practice of venerating idols, grounded in the Incarnation.

Illuminative Way: In Christian Mysticism, the second stage of progress, consisting in moments of union, insight, or vision.

Incarnation: In Christianity, the belief that the second person of the Trinity, the Son, became fully human, so that Jesus is both human and divine. Lesser realizations of "incarnation" are found in Judaism—as is some understandings of the *tzaddik*—and in Islam—as in the imam.

infallibility: An inability to be in error; a characteristic claimed by Shiite Muslims for the imam and by Roman Catholics since the 19th century for the bishop of Rome.

inspiration: The conviction that God's Holy Spirit can find expression through human words of the prophets or of Scriptures.

islama: Submission, from which the religion of Islam draws its name. Found already in Abraham the Righteous.

jihad: Literally, "to strive," with the meaning of "striving in the way of Allah," which includes waging war in defense of Islam.

Kabbalah: Literally, "tradition," the form of Jewish Mysticism, especially based in the *Zohar*, the *Book of Splendor*, that interpreted Torah in terms of exile and return to God.

kalam: In Islam, the application of reason to the truths of faith; theology.

kataphasis: In orthodox theology, the form of speech that makes positive affirmations, such as "God is good."

Lectio Divina: Latin phrase meaning "Holy Reading"; the meditative reading of Scripture characteristic of Western monks.

liturgy: From the Greek for "public work," the official worship of a religious community; in Christianity, it refers, above all, to the Eucharist (or Mass or Lord's Supper).

martyr: From the Greek word for witness, someone who endures death for the sake of a religious conviction. In Judaism, Rabbi Akiva died testifying to the oneness of God; in Christianity, Ignatius of Antioch died testifying to Christ; in Islam, Hussein died testifying to the prophetic principle embodied by 'Ali.

mendicant: A beggar. In Christianity, a member of a religious order dedicated to evangelical poverty; in Islam (see **dervish**).

merkabah: The "throne-chariot" of Ezekiel's vision of God that becomes the central symbol of Jewish Mysticism in the Rabbinic period.

Messiah: From the Hebrew for "anointed," a conviction shared by all three traditions concerning a redeemer/rescuer of God's people. For Jews, there have been a number of failed Messiahs, including Sabbatai Zevi; for Christians, Jesus is the Messiah; for Shiite Muslims, the return of the imam as Mahdi ("enlightened one") is messianic.

midrash: The process of interpretation of Torah that extends and contemporizes the ancient text. If applied to legal material, it is *halachic*; if applied to non-legal material, it is *haggadic*.

Mishnah: The codification of Jewish Law carried out by Judah ha-Nasi c. 200 C.E. on the basis of the interpretation of Torah.

Monasticism: From the Greek *monos* ("alone"), the oldest form of religious fellowship in Christianity, taking the forms of semi-eremitical and cenobite.

mysticism: In every religion, the effort or process aimed at a direct experience of, or union with, the divine (in Islam, *al-haqq*, the "real"), especially through prayer and contemplation—recollection.

New Testament: The 27 writings in Greek that constitute the Christian portion of the Bible, which encompasses also the writings found in the Greek version of the Hebrew Bible (TaNaK), now called the Old Testament by Christians.

opus dei: In Latin, the "work of God," also called the "Divine Office," referring to the round of prayer in monastic life consisting mainly of psalms.

orthodoxy: In Christianity, "right teaching," a title claimed by the Eastern Church (Greek/Russian Orthodoxy); in Judaism, the term refers more to right practice and is claimed by Orthodox Jews who continue the Talmudic tradition. In Islam, the Orthodox Caliphate refers to the caliphs up to and including 'Ali.

Passion: That part of the Gospel story that relates the suffering and death of Jesus; a main focus of meditation for medieval mystics in particular.

penitence: Remorse or sorrow for sins and a turning away from sin found in all three traditions: in Judaism, especially in the Pious Ones of Germany in the Middle Ages; in Christianity, through the entire history of asceticism; and in Islam, as one of the first stages of the Sufi path.

persecution: The effort to punish or eliminate a religious movement. Christians claim to have been persecuted by Jews in the beginning and, later, by Romans; Jews were persecuted sporadically by Christians throughout their history; Shiite Muslims claim a long history of persecution from the Sunni.

Pharisees: The sect in 1st-century Judaism whose commitment to the observance of Torah in all its Laws by all Jews became the basis for the oral Torah and the normative form of Judaism for two millennia.

pilgrimage: Physically, a journey to a place regarded as holy, such as the Hajj in Islam; metaphorically, the journey toward God through personal transformation.

Purgative Way: In Christian Mysticism, the first stage of mysticism, consisting in physical asceticism and control of the passions.

qasida: A pre-Islamic poetic form that provides motifs to Sufi mystics: the meeting and separation of lovers, a journey, and recollection of the beloved.

Qur'an: The Muslim Scripture, believed to be the literal word of Allah in Arabic. The Qur'an was revealed to Muhammad beginning at Mount Hira in 610, edited after the death of the Prophet, and arranged in 114 suras (sections).

rabbi: Literally, "great one," the teacher within the Jewish community whose work is based in observance of the Commandments of Torah.

recollection: The form of contemplative prayer particularly associated with 15th- and 16th-century Spanish Mysticism, emphasizing not a "going out" in ecstasy but a "gathering in" that focuses on inner unity with God.

reformation: In general, the effort to restore a religion to what is regarded as its true nature. In Christianity, the term is associated especially with the Protestant Reformation of the 16th century; in Judaism, with the Reform Judaism of the 19th and 20th centuries; and in Islam, with the 18th- and 19th-century movements begun by Wahhab and Sanusi.

sacrament: In the broad sense, a ritual sign that effects what it symbolizes. Christians recognize either seven such sacraments (Roman Catholics) or two (baptism and the Lord's Supper).

saint: In all three traditions, a human being who has achieved or attained a state of transformation that makes him or her "holy," or more like the divine.

salat: One of the five Pillars of Islam; prayer, whether in private or common, that consists of a series of prostrations facing Mecca (the *qiblah* means "orientation").

sanctification: The process by which humans grow more like God—holy—through God's empowerment.

sawm: In Islam, fasting for discipline and the study of Qur'an during the month of Ramadan; one of the five pillars of the religion.

scribes: "Men of the book" (*ha soferim*) whose ability at scriptural interpretation through midrash supported the religious commitments of the Pharisees.

sefirot: In classical Kabbalah, the emanations from the divine, 10 in number, that are found in the world, in the human body, and in Torah.

semi-eremitical: The form of Monasticism found among the desert fathers and in Eastern Orthodoxy; monks live mainly alone but meet for worship.

shahadah: The Islamic confession of faith: "I affirm that Allah alone is God, and I affirm that Muhammad is his prophet [*Rasul*]."

Shari'ah: From *shar*, "path," the system of law in Islam derived from the Qur'an and the Hadith of the Prophet. There are four distinct schools of legal interpretation: the Hanafi, Maliki, Shafi'i, and Hanbali.

shaykh: The leader of a Sufi fellowship (taquiya) who exercises absolute authority over those who are students (murid); assumed to have achieved an exalted state of sanctity.

Shiite: The minority sect within Islam, technically the *shiat' Ali* ("the party of 'Ali"), which recognizes only imams descended from the son-in-law and cousin of the Prophet as the legitimate source of authority and which reads the tradition esoterically.

shirk: In Islam, the opposite of righteous submission to Allah: forgetfulness, neglect, disobedience, giving partners to Allah.

Shiur Koma: Literally, "measure of the body," a feature of Merkabah Mysticism consisting in speculation on the divine body; also plays a role in Kabbalism.

Shoah: The Holocaust; term used for the murder of some 6 million Jews by the Nazis in the mid-20th century.

sin: In Judaism and Christianity, the deliberate rejection of God's will through disobedience; in Islam, the term is *shirk*.

stages (or **stations**): The steps that a Sufi can accomplish through human effort: repentance, renunciation, watchfulness, and so on.

states: Conditions that a Sufi cannot bring about but are given by Allah, such as fana ("annihilation") or *flashes* (illuminations).

Sufi: In Islam, one dedicated to the path of union with Allah or *al-haqq*, a path of knowledge, love, and prayer.

Sufism: The term describes everything involved in the Sufi way of life as it has existed in the history of Islam.

Sunni: The majority version of Islam, based on the Sunna, the custom of the Prophet.

sura: The name for each of the 114 divisions of the Qur'an, which after the first (*Fatihah* means "opening"), run from the longest to the shortest.

Talmud: The compilation of rabbinic lore in two forms: the Talmud of the Land of Israel (4th century) and the Babylonian Talmud (5th–6th centuries), with the latter being more authoritative. Both add Gemara (Aramaic discussion) to the Mishnah (Hebrew statement of Law).

TaNaK: An acronym describing the contents of the Hebrew Bible: Torah, Neviim (Prophets), and Ketuvim (Writings).

Tannaim: From the verb "to repeat," the first generations of those handing down the midrashic traditions that form rabbinic Judaism, including such figures as Yochanan ben Zakkai and Akiva.

Tawhid: The divine unity in Islam, which in some Sufi speculation turns out to be something close to Pantheism or, perhaps, Panentheism.

theology: The classical definition is "faith seeking understanding"; the use of human reason in investigating and interrogating the belief of a religious community.

theosis: Greek term meaning the process of divinization; thought to be possible in Greek Orthodoxy because of a conviction that grace gives a "participation in divine nature," which is realized through the practice of the spiritual life.

theosophy: In the study of mysticism, the construction of reality found in a mystic or mystical school, sometimes based on visions.

tikkun: In Kabbalism, "mending the world" (*tikkun ha-olam*) is the task of Israel by observance of the Commandments and, especially, the task of the mystics, who accomplish unity (*devequt*) with the divine through their prayerful "attention" (*kawwanah*) and speed the process of cosmic healing.

Torah: The most inclusive symbol for God's word in Judaism. Refers, first, to the five books of Moses in TaNaK; then, to all of Scripture; then, to all the tradition embracing the faithful interpretation of Torah in the community.

Trinity: In Christian theology, the understanding that there is only one God and that this same God subsists in three "persons": Father, Son, and Holy Spirit.

tzaddik: Within the Hasidic movement, the head of a community, not because of learning in the Law but because of personal holiness and charismatic power.

Unitive Way: In Christian Mysticism, the final stage of progress, "spiritual marriage" between the soul and God, characterized by great peace and with a simple accessibility to all things.

zakat: In Islam, one of the five pillars, the poor-tax; a portion of one's goods yearly is dedicated to the poor and needy.

zawiya: The room, sometimes found in a mosque, where the members of a Sufi brotherhood meet for study and prayer.

Zohar: The *Book of Splendor*, the central text of Kabbalism, holding a canonical position within the tradition.

Bibliography

Essential Reading:

Readings from the Bible are from the Revised Standard Version, found in *The New Oxford Annotated Bible: Revised Standard Edition*. Edited by H. G. May and B. M. Metzger. New York: Oxford University Press, 1978. Readings from the Qur'an are from *The Meaning of the Glorious Koran, An Explanatory Translation*. Mohammed Marmaduke Pickthall. New York: Mentor Books, 1953. Although somewhat difficult, it is praised for its accuracy in rendering the Arabic. More accessible is *The Qur'an Translation*. Abdullah Yusuf Ali. New York: Thrike Tarsile Qur'an, Inc., 2007.

I have made particularly heavy use of the introductions, translations, and notes found in the monumental series, *The Classics of Western Spirituality*. R. J. Payne, ed., et. al. New York: Paulist Press, 1978–2007. It makes available new (sometimes the first) translations into English of authors from the Jewish, Christian, and Muslim traditions—as well as others. I list below the specific volumes used in the lectures. Further resources are available for questions of religion in general in a volume edited by M. Eliade, *The Encyclopedia of Religion*. 16 vols. New York: MacMillan, 1986.

For three distinct traditions see J. Neusner and A. J. Avery, eds. *The Routledge Dictionary of Judaism*. New York: Routledge, 2004; F. L. Cross. *The Oxford Dictionary of the Christian Church*. 3rd ed. Edited by E. A. Livingstone. New York: Oxford University Press, 1997; and J. L. Esposito. *The Oxford Dictionary of Islam*. New York: Oxford University Press, 2003.

On the topic of mysticism in general, one can consult E. Underhill's classic (but dated) *Mysticism: A Study in the Nature and Development of Man's Spiritual Consciousness*. New York: E.P. Dutton, 1911; and E. Underhill's *The Essentials of Mysticism and Other Essays*. New York: E.P. Dutton, 1960; as well as the more recent collection of essays edited by R. Woods, *Understanding Mysticism*. Garden City, New York: Image Books, 1980. For guidance to each tradition of mysticism, see G. Scholem's *Major Trends in Jewish Mysticism*. New York: Schocken Books, 1941; B. McGinn's *The Presence of God: A History of Western Christian Mysticism*. 4 vols. New York: Crossroad, 1991–2005; and S.H. Nasr's *Islamic Spirituality*. 2 vols. (*World Spirituality*). New York: Crossroad, 1991.

Recommended Reading:

Allen, R. S., trans. *Richard Rolle*. In *The Classics of Western Spirituality*. New York: Paulist Press, 1988. A fine collection of writings from the hermit of Hamphole, whose prose and poetry exemplify 14th-century English mysticism.

Armstrong, R. J. and I. C. Brady, trans. *Francis and Clare*. In *The Classics of Western Spirituality*. New York: Paulist Press, 1982. This volume contains the most important writings of the founders of the Franciscans and the Poor Clares.

Attar, Farid ad-Din. *Muslim Saints and Mystics*. Translated by J. Alberry. London: Routledge and Kegan Paul, 1966. A selection of encomia from the author of the authoritative account of early Sufi saints like Rabia'.

Austin, R. W. J., trans. *Ibn al-Arabi*. In *The Classics of Western Spirituality*. New York: Paulist Press, 1980. This edition of the *Bezels of Wisdom* also provides an introduction and notes that place al-Arabi among the great Gnostic Sufis.

Bamberger, J. E., trans. *Evagrius Ponticus, The Praktikos and Chapters on Prayer*. In *Cistercian Studies* 4. Kalamazoo, MI: Cistercian Publications, 1981. A translation of the 4th-century writer's key works together with an introduction and notes.

Band, A. J., ed. *Nahum of Bratslav*. In *The Classics of Western Spirituality*. New York: Paulist Press, 1978. This volume contains a selection of the tales for which the Hasidic movement was renowned.

Berthold, G. C., trans. *Maximus Confessor*. In *The Classics of Western Spirituality*. New York: Paulist Press, 1985. The introduction places the great defender of the orthodox faith in historical context.

Bokser, B. Z., trans. *The Talmud: Selected Writings*. In *The Classics of Western Spirituality*. New York: Paulist Press, 1989. This anthology provides a sample of texts from the classic source for Rabbinic Judaism.

Buber, M. *I and Thou*. Translated by R. G. Smith. New York: Charles Scribner's Sons, 1958. The classic statement of a form of mysticism written by a Jew who was thoroughly at home in contemporary philosophy.

———. *Tales of the Hasidim: The Later Masters*. New York: Schocken, 1948. The pioneer in the study of the Hasidic movement makes available a selection of the tales that characterize a major feature of the movement.

Bynum, C. W. *Jesus as Mother: Studies in the Spirituality of the High Middle Ages*. Berkeley: University of California Press, 1982. The author examines the boldness on vision and theological expression of mystics such as Julian of Norwich.

Cadavid, L., trans. *Two Who Attained: Twentieth Century Sufi Saints*. Louisville: Fons Vitae, 2005. This book makes available the witness of al-Alawi and Fatimah Yashrutiyya in an attractive translation.

Calvin, J. *Institutes of the Christian Religion*. 2 vols. Translated by J. Allen. Philadelphia: Presbyterian Board of Publishing, 1813. The classic work of reformed theology, with attacks on Catholic institutions and positive prescriptions for Christian life.

Carroll, T. K., ed. *Jeremy Taylor*. In *The Classics of Western Spirituality*. New York: Paulist Press, 1990. The two classic works— *Holy Living* and *Holy Dying*—of the Anglican Divine are accompanied by an introduction and notes.

Chamberas, P. A., trans. *Nicodemos of the Holy Mountain*. In *The Classics of Western Spirituality*. New York: Paulist Press, 1989. The central role of the "Jesus Prayer" is especially clear in the writings of this master of the Hesychastic tradition.

Charlesworth, C. H., ed. *The Old Testament Pseudepigrapha*. 2 vols. Garden City, New York: Doubleday, 1983–85. Complete collection of Jewish apocrypha, including 1 Enoch and 3 Enoch, cited in the lectures.

Chittick, W. C. and P. L. Wilson, trans. *Fahkruddin Iraqi*. In *The Classics of Western Spirituality*. New York: Paulist Press, 1982. A solid introduction, notes, and translation of the Sufi poet in the Persian language.

Clark, J. P. H. and R. Dorwwod, trans. *Walter Hilton*. In *The Classics of Western Spirituality*. New York: Paulist Press, 1991. This edition of the *Scale of Perfection* is accompanied by an introduction and helpful notes.

Colledge, E. and B. McGinn, trans. *Meister Eckhard*. In *The Classics of Western Spirituality*. New York: Paulist Press, 1981. The most difficult and controversial of the Dominican mystics of the Rhineland is represented by his relatively accessible sermons.

Colledge, E. and J. Walsh, trans. *Julian of Norwich*. In *The Classics of Western Spirituality*. New York: Paulist Press, 1978. A fine edition of the *Showings* from one of the greatest female mystics of the medieval period.

Colledge, W. *The Medieval Mystics of England*. New York: Charles Scribner's Sons, 1961. A brief introduction of and selection from each of the great mystics of the English middle ages.

Cousins, E., trans. *Bonaventure*. In *The Classics of Western Spirituality*. New York: Paulist Press, 1978. Together with introduction and notes, this volume contains the most important spiritual writings of the Franciscan master.

Crouver, D. and G. Christianson, trans. *The Spirituality of the German Awakening*. In *The Classics of Western Spirituality*. New York: Paulist Press, 2003. A fascinating collection of texts from Lutheran pastors seeking to make Christianity respond to modernity in the 19th century.

Cupitt, D. *Mysticism after Modernity: Religion and Spirituality in the Modern World*. Malden, MA: Blackwell, 1998. An intelligent but ultimately reductionistic rendering of mysticism in the context of modern thought.

Dan, J. trans. *The Early Kabbalah*. In *The Classics of Western Spirituality*. New York: Paulist Press, 1986. This volume pulls together texts that are otherwise difficult to find and places them in an intelligible narrative of development.

Danner, V., and W. M. Thackston, trans. *Ibn 'Ata' Illah/Kwaja Abdullah Ansari*. In *The Classics of Western Spirituality*. New York: Paulist Press, 1978. This volume contains the first author's *Book of Wisdom* and the second author's *Intimate Conversation*.

Dervish, H. M. B. *Journeys with a Sufi Master*. London: Octagon, 1982. An uncritical but fascinating treatment of Idries Shah by an admirer.

Erb, P., trans. *Jacob Boehme*. In *The Classics of Western Spirituality*. New York: Paulist Press, 1978. A selection of texts that show the distinctive character of this German Lutheran Gnostic.

Fine, L., trans. *Safed Spirituality*. In *The Classics of Western Spirituality*. New York: Paulist Press, 1984. The introduction provides the historical and literary context for the form of mysticism that arose among Isaac Luria and his associates.

Ganes, G. E., ed. *Ignatius of Loyola*. In *The Classics of Western Spirituality*. New York: Paulist Press, 1991. The *Spiritual Exercises*, together with an introduction and notes.

Gibson, C. S., trans. "John Cassian." In *Nicene and Post-Nicene Fathers*. Edited by P. Shaff and H. Ware, 2nd series, 11. Peabody, MA: Hendrickson, 1994 [1894]. A complete edition of Casssian's *Institutes* and *Conferences*.

Giles, M. E., trans. *Francisco de Osuna*. In *The Classics of Western Spirituality*. New York: Paulist Press, 1981. The *Third Spiritual Alphabet*, with its teaching on recollection, had a profound impact on Teresa of Avila.

Goodenough, E. R. *By Light, Light: The Mystic Gospel of Hellenistic Judaism*. New Haven: Yale University Press, 1963. Advances the argument that Philo of Alexandria represents a mysticism within Judaism that was prevalent in the Diaspora.

Green, A., trans. *Menahum Nahum of Chernobyl*. In *The Classics of Western Spirituality*. New York: Paulist Press, 1982. The author is an example of the mainstreaming of the Hasidic movement within the longer tradition of Jewish spirituality.

Gregg, R. C., trans. *Athanasius*. In *The Classics of Western Spirituality*. New York: Paulist Press, 1980. Makes available a translation of the *Life of Antony* by the great Alexandrian bishop and defender of orthodoxy.

Hammer, R., trans. *The Classic Midrash: Tannaitic Commentaries on the Bible*. In *The Classics of Western Spirituality*. New York: Paulist Press, 1995. The interpretation of the Torah is the heart of the Rabbinic tradition. This volume makes some of the earliest examples of midrash accessible.

Harris, M. J., ed. *Birgitta of Sweden*. In *The Classics of Western Spirituality*. Translated by A. R. Keyel. New York: Paulist Press, 1990. A selection of visionary and epistolary texts from the itinerant visionary.

Hart, C., trans. *Hadewijch*. In *The Classics of Western Spirituality*. New York: Paulist Press, 1980. Little is known of the Beguine, but the extant poetry and letters show a passionate nature and mystical impulse.

Hart, C. and J. Bishop. *Hildegard of Bingen*. In *The Classics of Western Spirituality*. New York: Paulist Press, 1990. Text and illustrations from the medieval Benedictine visionary, with a helpful introduction and notes.

Hasbrouk, J. B., trans. *William of St. Thierry, Exposition on the Epistle to the Romans.* In *Cistercian Studies* 27. Kalamazoo, MI: Cistercian Publications, 1980. The devotee of Saint Bernard shows how scriptural exposition turns to prayer within the monastic tradition of reading the "sacred page."

Heschel, A. *God in Search of Man: a Philosophy of Judaism.* New York: Farrar, Strauss and Cudahay, 1955. The title is revealing: The emphasis is not on mystical ascent, but on God's love for humanity and for human justice.

———. *The Prophets.* New York: Harper and Row, 1962. A masterful treatment of the biblical prophets by a Jew whose thought emerges from tradition and addresses the contemporary world.

Hitti, P. K. *Islam: A Way of Life.* Chicago: Regnery Gateway, 1970. As the title suggests, this introduction emphasizes the Islamic tradition as a living religion.

Homerin, Th. Emil, trans. *'Umar ibn al-Farid.* In *The Classics of Western Spirituality.* New York: Paulist Press, 2001. A fresh poetic rendering of the great Sufi poet of North Africa, together with an introduction and notes.

Jacob, L. *Jewish Mystical Testimonies.* New York: Schocken Books, 1976. A fine collection of short primary texts, with introductions and notes from the earliest to latest periods of Jewish Mysticism.

Jeffrey, A., ed. *Islam: Muhammad and his Religion.* The Library of the Liberal Arts. New York: Bobbs-Merrill, 1958. The basic elements of Islam are illustrated by copious citations from primary texts.

Johnson, L. T. *The Writings of the New Testament: An Interpretation.* 2nd ed. Minneapolis: Fortress Press, 1999. Treats the writings of the New Testament in their historical context, literary form and religious purpose.

Kavanaugh, K., ed. *John of the Cross* . In *The Classics of Western Spirituality.* New York: Paulist Press, 1987. Readings from each of the major works of the great Spanish mystic of the 16th century are accompanied by helpful notes.

Kavanaugh, K., trans. *Teresa of Avila (The Classics of Western Spirituality).* New York: Paulist Press, 1979. This edition of *The*

Interior Castle makes evident the humor, charm, and profundity of the great Spanish mystic of the 16th century.

————, trans. *Israel Horowitz: The Generations of Adam*. In *The Classics of Western Spirituality*. New York: :Paulist Press, 1996. This first section of a much more massive work shows the way that Lurianic Kabbalism influenced subsequent Jewish literature.

Krey, P. D. W. and P. D. S. Krey, trans. *Luther's Spirituality*. In *The Classics of Western Spirituality*. New York: Paulist Press, 2007. A fine collection of Luther's pastoral writings, showing what is new and what is traditional in his spirituality.

Lawrence, B. B., trans. *Nizam ad-Din Awliya*. In *The Classics of Western Spirituality*. New York: Paulist Press, 1992. An edition that places the moral discourses of this Indian Sufi into historical and social context.

Layton. B., ed. *The Gnostic Scriptures*. Garden City, New York: Doubleday, 1987. The most important of the 2nd-century Christian phenomenon are here made available, together with helpful annotations.

Liechtz, D., trans. *Early Anabaptist Spirituality*. In *The Classics of Western Spirituality*. New York: Paulist Press, 1994. The introduction and notes place these valuable testimonies into their historical context of radical reformation.

Lings, M. *A Sufi Saint of the Twentieth Century: Shaikh Ahmed al-Alawi*. 2nd ed. Berkeley: University of California Press, 1971. A sympathetic and thorough examination of the 20th-century North African head of a Sufi brotherhood; includes the first-person account of M. Carret.

Luibheid, C., trans. *Pseudo-Dionysius*. In *The Classics of Western Spirituality*. New York: Paulist Press, 1987. The key works of the writer influential on both Eastern and Western spirituality in his emphasis on the apophantic way.

Luibheid, C. and N. Russell, trans. *John Climacus*. In *The Classics of Western Spirituality*. New York: Paulist Press, 1982. Introduction and notes accompany this translation of the abbot whose *Ladder* was perhaps the most-read book in the Orthodox tradition.

Luther, M. *Three Treatises*. Translated by M. Jacobs. Philadelphia: Fortress Press, 1970. This volume contains the two treatises, *Letter to the German Nobility* and *The Babylonian Captivity of the Church*, discussed in the lectures.

Malherbe, A. J. and E. Ferguson, trans. *Gregory of Nyssa*. In *The Classics of Western Spirituality*. New York: Paulist Press, 1992. Introduction and notes to his *Life of Moses*.

Maloney, G. A., trans. *Pseudo-Macarius*. In *The Classics of Western Spirituality*. New York: Paulist Press, 1992. Introduction and notes to the translation of key works by the figure of key importance in the development of mysticism in Eastern Christianity.

Matt, D. C., trans. *Zohar, the Book of Splendor*. In *The Classics of Western Spirituality*. New York: Paulist Press, 1983. An accessible translation of the classic text of Kabbalism together with a helpful introduction and notes.

Merton, T. *The New Man*. New York: Mentor Image, 1961. One among many writers who show the trappist monks' immersion in the long tradition of monastic spirituality as well as his contemporary sensibility.

———. *Raids on the Unspeakable*. New York: New Directions, 1964. A slender volume that exemplifies the "turn to the world" of the iconic 20th-century mystic.

Meyendorff, J., trans. *Gregory Palamas*. In *The Classics of Western Spirituality*. New York: Paulist Press, 1983. Introduction and notes accompany this fresh translation of the *Triads*, a key work in the development of Hesychasm.

Nasr, S. H. *Ideals and Realities of Islam*. Boston: Beacon Press, 1966. A scholarly work that is also written from the "inside" of the Islamic reality.

Neusner, J. *The Way of Torah: An Introduction to Judaism*. 4th ed. Belmont: Wordsworth, 1988. A world-renowned expert in the field covers the basics of this religious tradition at the collegiate level.

Nicholson, R. A. *The Mystics of Islam*. London: Routledge and Kegan, 1914. A short and masterful exposition of the basics of Sufism, richly supported by primary texts.

Noffke, S., trans. *Catherine of Sienna*. In *The Classics of Western Spirituality*. New York: Paulist Press, 1980. The reasons for the saint's being designated a "doctor of the church" are abundantly displayed in this volume.

Norris, K. *The Cloister Walk*. New York: Riverhead Books, 1996. An example of contemporary lay Catholic spirituality shaped by contact with the Benedictine tradition.

Palladius. *The Lausiac History* (*Ancient Christian Writers* 34). Translated by R. T. Meyer. New York: Newman Press, 1964. The firsthand account of the monks of the desert by a bishop and monk who spent years visiting them and gathering their stories.

Pentovsky, A., ed. *The Pilgrim's Tale*. In *The Classics of Western Spirituality*. New York: Paulist Press, 1999. The tangled development of this fascinating apology for the *Philocalia* and the "Jesus Prayer" is dissected in this volume.

Peters, F. E. *Children of Abraham: Judaism, Christianity, Islam*. Princeton: Princeton University Press, 1982. A good comparison of the three traditions, hitting both elements of similarity and distinctiveness.

Rahman, F. *Islam*. Garden City, New York: Anchor Books, 1968. A scholarly treatment of the religion that uses modern historiography yet is respectful of tradition.

Renard, J., trans. *Ibn Abbad of Ronda*. In *The Classics of Western Spirituality*. New York: Paulist Press, 1986. A fine collection of the North African Sufi's didactic writings.

Renard, J., trans. *Knowledge of God in Classical Sufism*. In *The Classics of Western Spirituality*. New York: Paulist Press 2004. A collection of Sufi texts that are organized not by author but by the central issue of the knowledge of God attained by mystics.

Rubenstein, R. L. *After Auschwitz: Radical Theology and Contemporary Judaism*. New York: Bobbs-Merrill, 1966. Takes the *Shoah* as threatening to all classic forms of Jewish theology and life.

Savage, A. and N. Watson, trans. *Anchorite Spirituality*. In *The Classics of Western Spirituality*. New York: Paulist Press, 1991. This volume contains the advice given by male directors to female anchoresses in medieval England. Noteworthy is the full text of *Ancrene Wisse*.

Scholem, G. *Origins of the Kabbalah*. Translated by A. Arkech. Edited by R. J. Z. Werblowsky. Princeton: Princeton University Press, 1962. The great student of Jewish mysticism takes on the puzzle of the historical sources and origin of the movement that defined the tradition for centuries.

———. *Sabbatai Zevi: The Mystical Messiah, 1626–1676*. Princeton: Princeton University Press, 1973. Classic historical treatment of the most controversial figure in Jewish mysticism.

Sells, M. A. *Early Islamic Mysticism*. In *The Classics of Western Spirituality*. New York: Paulist Press, 1996. A collection of texts, with notes and an introduction, that shows how vibrant and intellectually challenging Sufism was from its inception.

Shah, I., *The Sufis*. London: W. H. Allen, 1964. An influential book that advances the case for Sufism being larger and more universal than Islam.

Shrady, M., trans. *Johannes Tauler*. In *The Classics of Western Spirituality*. New York: Paulist Press, 1985. A fresh translation of sermons from the great Rhineland mystic whom Luther thought the best of preachers.

Stanwood, P. G., ed. *William Law*. In *The Classics of Western Spirituality*. New York: Paulist Press, 1978. A useful edition of the works of this classic and beloved Anglican writer whose good sense is much valued.

Teilhard, P. De Chardin. *The Future of Man*. New York: Harper and Row, 1964. A collection of essays that puts the evolutionary mystic's ideas in accessible form.

———. *Hymn of the Universe*. New York: Harper and Row, 1965. Together with *The Divine Milieu*, the work of the Jesuit mystic that is most explicitly connected to his Christian faith.

Thomas á Kempis. *The Imitation of Christ*. Translated by L. Sherley-Price. London: Penguin Books, 1952. The Christian writing that had a profound impact on later mystics, e.g., Ignatius of Loyola, and on ordinary believers down to the present.

Tobin, F., trans. *Henry Suso*. In *The Classics of Western Spirituality*. New York: Paulist Press, 1989. This edition is valuable for its inclusion of the materials that give insight into the personal spiritual development of this most self-revealing of the Rhineland mystics.

———, trans. *Mechtild of Magdeberg*. In *The Classics of Western Spirituality*. New York: Paulist Press, 1998. The texts of the Beguine, amplified by an introduction and notes, help fill out the picture of female mystics within Christianity and their use of courtly literature.

Vermes, G. *The Dead Sea Scrolls in English*, 2nd ed. New York: Penguin Books, 1975. A readable version of the Essene texts, with a helpful introduction and notes.

Waddell, H., trans. *The Desert Fathers*. Ann Arbor, MI: University of Michigan Press, 1936. This volume makes available several compositions originating in the monks of the Egyptian wilderness of the 4th century.

Walsh, K., trans. *Bernard of Clairvaux, On the Song of Songs*. 4 vols. In *Cistercian Studies* 4. Kalamazoo, MI: Cistercian Publications, 1981. The tradition of monastic spirituality with its multi-level interpretation of Scripture is well displayed in the work of the great Cistercian abbot.

Walsh, K., trans. *The Cloud of Unknowing*. In *The Classics of Western Spirituality*. New York: Paulist Press, 1981. The great apophantic witness of 14th-century England, deeply marked by Pseudo-Dionysius, but marvelously alive in its insight.

Watt, W. M. *Muhammad, Prophet and Statesman*. Oxford: Oxford University Press, 1961. A straightforward biography using the best in historical methods, and respectful of the prophet's accomplishments.

Weil, S. *Waiting for God*. Translated by E. Craufurd. New York: Harper and Row, 1951. The collection of short writings that best communicates her mystical understanding on the fringes of Christianity.

Weiner, H. *9 ½ Mystics: The Kabbalah Today*. New York: Holt, Rinehart and Winston, 1969. A first-person account of various forms of contemporary Jewish Mysticism, with fascinating personal profiles.

Whaling, F., ed. *John and Charles Wesley*. In *The Classics of Western Spirituality*. New York: Paulist Press, 1981. Key texts from John Wesley, founder of the Methodists, and a generous selection of hymns from his brother, Charles.

Wiesel, E. *The Gates of the Forest*. Translated by F. Frenaye. New York: Avon, 1966. A post-holocaust book by the Nobel-prize-winning survivor of the camps, which opens with a Hasidic tale.

Windeatt, B. A., trans. *The Book of Margery Kempe*. London: Penguin Books, 1985. The fascinating first example of an English autobiography as dictated by an illiterate but highly expressive mystic.

Zinn, G. A., trans. *Richard of St. Victor*. In *The Classics of Western Spirituality*. New York: Paulist Press, 1979. This volume contains both portions of the Victorine's great mystical treatise, which brings close psychological analysis to the life of prayer.

Zion, B. Z., trans. *Abraham Isaac Kook*. In *The Classics of Western Spirituality*. New York: Paulist Press, 1978. The introduction places this attractive representative of modern Jewish Mysticism in historical context and provides a translation of major works.

Notes

Notes